Poles Apart

The international reporting of climate scepticism

James Painter

REUTERS
INSTITUTE for the
STUDY of
JOURNALISM

UNIVERSITY OF
OXFORD

The Reuters Institute for the Study of Journalism is very grateful to the following organisations for funding this study:

The British Council
The European Climate Foundation
The Grantham Research Institute on Climate Change and the Environment, London School of Economics and Political Science

Contents

List of Figures

List of Tables

Executive Summary

This is a wide-ranging comparative study about the prevalence of climate sceptic voices in the print media in six countries: Brazil, China, France, India, the United Kingdom, and the United States of America. More than 3,000 articles taken from two newspapers in each of the six countries were analysed over two separate three-month periods in 2007 and 2009/10. A further 1,900 articles were examined from the eight other national British newspapers over the same periods to give a more comprehensive picture of climate scepticism in the UK print media.

The main aims of the study were to track any increase in the amount of space given to sceptical voices over the two periods and to map significant differences both between countries and within the print media of the same country. Because we were also interested in exploring whether there was a correspondence between the prevalence of sceptical voices and the political leaning of a newspaper, an example of a left-leaning and a right-leaning newspaper were selected in most countries.

Before the content analysis, *Poles Apart* gives an overview of climate scepticism in different countries, and particularly in the USA, and suggests that it is predominately an Anglo-Saxon phenomenon. It then surveys past research on the prevalence of scepticism in the media around the world, again drawing a distinction between countries like the USA, the UK, and Australia, where it has often been present in parts of the media, and the developing world and continental Europe where it has been largely absent.

Poles Apart goes to considerable lengths to describe the large variety of types of climate-sceptical voices that exist: from those who are sceptical that the world is warming, to those who are sceptical about the influence of humans in the warming, to those who are sceptical about the pace and extent of its impacts, to those who are sceptical about whether urgent action and government spending are necessary to combat it. The analysis attempted to separate the different types of sceptical voices, their background (professional or otherwise), and in which part of a newspaper they were most likely to appear.

The main findings of the content analysis from the six-country comparative study are the following.

1

First, the absolute number of articles which included sceptical voices increased for all but one (*Le Monde* in France) of the twelve newspapers over the two periods. However, expressed as a percentage of all the articles covering climate change or global warming, there were wide regional variations: strong increases in the case of the UK and US press, compared to mild increases or falls in Brazil, China, India, and France.

Second, other substantial cross-country differences exist, endorsing the view that climate scepticism is much more widespread in UK and US newspapers than in the other four countries.

- In general the UK and the US print media quoted or mentioned significantly more sceptical voices than the other four countries. Together they represented more than 80% of the times such voices were quoted across all six countries.

- Over 40% of the articles where such voices were included were to be found in the opinion pages and editorials as compared to the news pages. But the print media in Brazil, China, India, and France had many fewer such pieces than those in the UK and the USA.

- Politicians represented around a third of all the sceptical voices quoted or mentioned, compared to the lower share (about a fifth) of university climate scientists. But the UK and American newspapers were much more likely to quote politicians than the newspapers in other countries. The four Anglo-Saxon newspapers accounted for 86% of all the times politicians were quoted. France was the only other country to quote national politicians, whilst the other three countries either quoted none or politicians from other countries.

- The sceptics who question the role that human factors play in global warming had a higher incidence in the print media in Brazil, China, India, and France, representing nearly 90% of the sceptics quoted or mentioned. This compared with a figure of around 60% for the USA and the UK.

Third, there is strong evidence that in the countries where sceptical voices appear in greater numbers, they are more likely to be found in right-leaning than left-leaning print media. In Brazil, France, and India, where few sceptic voices appear, there was little or no difference in the prevalence of sceptical viewpoints between the two print media chosen. However, in the case of the Anglophone countries, there does seem to be a correspondence between the perspective of a newspaper and the prevalence of sceptical voices:

- Over the two periods, in percentage terms in the UK, the left-leaning *Guardian/Observer* had fewer articles with sceptical voices than the right-leaning *Daily* and *Sunday Telegraph* (11% compared to 19%), despite the former's extensive coverage of 'Climategate'. In the USA, the *NYT* had slightly less than the *WSJ* (25% compared to 28%).

- However, the distinction is much more marked in the opinion pieces and editorials. The *Telegraphs* and *WSJ* had considerably more uncontested sceptical opinion pieces and/or editorials than the *Guardian* and *NYT*. For example, in the second period the *Guardian* had 11 opinion pieces including sceptical voices, but 9 of them were essentially dismissive of sceptical views. In contrast, the *Daily/Sunday Telegraph* included 24 opinion pieces of which over half expressed an essentially sceptical viewpoint. Likewise, over the two periods, in all of the opinion pieces in the *NYT* containing sceptical voices, the author disputed climate scepticism or rejected it. In contrast, of the 17 opinion pieces found in the *WSJ*, only one fitted this category.

The main findings from the study of ten UK national newspapers can be summarised thus:

- In general, the data suggests a strong correspondence between the perspective of a newspaper and the prevalence of sceptical voices within it, particularly on the opinion pages. By most measures (but not all), the more right-leaning tend to have more such voices, the left-leaning less.

- Over the two periods, in all ten newspapers there was an increase both in the absolute numbers of articles with sceptical voices in them and the percentage of articles with sceptical voices in them. However, the increase in the number of voices was most marked for the right-leaning *Express, Mail,* and *Star.* These were also the three newspapers that in the second period had the highest percentage figures. The *Express* had the most at 50% of all its articles quoting or mentioning sceptics, followed by the *Mail* (48%) and the *Star* (39%). This contrasted with the *Mirror* at 13%.

- Sceptical voices got a considerable airing in opinion pieces and editorials in all ten newspapers, although it is clearly more marked in some newspapers than others. Expressed as a percentage of the total number of articles mentioning climate change or global warming, in period 2 the *Sun* had the highest percentage (more than half), followed by the *Telegraph*, the *Express*, *The Times*, and the *Mail*. All five are right-leaning.

- The three more left-leaning newspapers (*Guardian, Independent*, and *Mirror*) had the lowest percentages of uncontested opinion pieces and editorials quoting sceptics; between them they had only 10 of the opinion pieces by sceptical authors of the total of 70 over the two periods; and they had no editorials quoting sceptical voices which were left uncontested.

- The right-wing *Express* newspapers in particular stood out for including sceptical voices: in the second period, it had the highest percentage of articles which included sceptical voices, the highest number of sceptical voices quoted or mentioned in its news reporting (more than any broadsheet), the highest number of direct quotes from sceptics, the highest number of editorials questioning the mainstream consensus, and the highest number of sceptical opinion pieces of any tabloid.

- The Global Warming Policy Foundation (GWPF) has been particularly successful in getting its views reported across most of the 10 newspapers. The two most quoted sceptics by far in the second period were Lord Lawson and Benny Peiser (more than 80 times between them), both from the GWPF. This compares with the 13 times for the most quoted climate-sceptic scientist (Professor Ian Plimer).

The content analysis did not set out to explain the differences between countries and within them. However, the wider analysis in the individual country studies suggests that the presence or absence of sceptical voices is determined by a complex mix of processes within newspapers (such as political ideology, journalistic practices, editorial culture, or the influence of editors and proprietors) and external societal forces (in particular the presence of sceptical political parties, the power of sceptical lobbying groups, the public profile of sceptical scientists, a country's energy matrix, the presence of web-based scepticism, or even a country's direct experience of a changing climate).

The weight of this study would suggest that, out of this wide range of factors, the presence of politicians espousing some variation of climate scepticism, the existence of organised interests that feed sceptical coverage, and partisan media receptive to this message, all play a particularly significant role in explaining the greater prevalence of sceptical voices in the print media of the USA and the UK. In these two countries climate change has become (to different degrees) more of a politicised issue, which politically polarised print media pick up on and reflect. This helps to explain why Brazil, India, France, and other countries in continental Europe have (to different degrees) a politically divided print media, but do not have the same prevalence of sceptical voices.

1. Poles Apart

On 28 June 2011 a special briefing was given to the media by the National Climatic Data Center (NCDC) in the USA to mark its annual State of the Climate report. Its main message was that the world's climate was not only continuing to warm, but was adding heat-trapping greenhouse gases even faster than in the past.[1] Amongst those giving the briefing was scientist Walt Meier from the University of Colorado who warned that 'the Arctic was changing faster than most of the rest of the world'.[2] The NCDC chart (Figure 1.1) shows that in 2010 average air temperatures over parts of Greenland and north-west Canada were at least five degrees above the norm for 1961–90, and among the highest increases above the norm for anywhere in the world.[3] The NCDC reported that 'among Canada's climate regions, the Arctic Tundra, Arctic Mountain and Fjords, and the Northwestern Forest all had their warmest winter on record'. Research suggests that 2010 was not a one-off event, as there has been a longer trend of warming in the Arctic in the last 60 years.[4]

So the Arctic and parts of the Antarctic are different from the rest of the world in terms of the magnitude of the warming to which they are being exposed. But even a glance at the coverage of climate change or global warming[5] in the international media in the same week reveals just how 'poles apart' or polarised the issue has become – at least in some countries – in the world of media, politics, and popular opinion. To label

[1] Randolph E. Schmid, 'Global Warming Continues as Greenhouse Gas Grows', Associated Press, 28 June 2011: http://abcnews.go.com/Technology/wireStory?id=13949844.
[2] A similar point was included in an article published on the same day by the Yale University's Environment 360 website: 'A World Centered on Sea Ice is Changing Swiftly at the Poles'. In the article, its senior editor Fen Montaigne wrote that 'as temperatures rise in the Arctic and along the Antarctic Peninsula faster than anywhere else on earth, evidence is growing that the sea ice's retreat is altering a food chain that supports a wide array of marine life, from single-celled phytoplankton to gray whales'. See http://e360.yale.edu/feature/a_world_centered_on_sea_ice_is_changing_swiftly_at_ the_poles/2420/.
[3] NCDC, State of the Climate Global Analysis 2010: www.ncdc.noaa.gov/sotc/global/2010/13.
[4] Darrell S. Kaufman et al, 'Recent Warming Reverses Long-Term Arctic Cooling', Science 325 (2009): 1236-1239.
[5] There is a difference in the meaning of the terms, although this study at times uses one of them as shorthand for both. According to the Pew Center in the USA, 'global warming' refers to the gradual increase of the Earth's average surface temperature, due to a build-up of greenhouse gases in the atmosphere. 'Climate change' is a broader term that refers to long-term changes in climate, including average temperature and precipitation, as well as changes in the seasonal or geographic variability of temperature and precipitation.

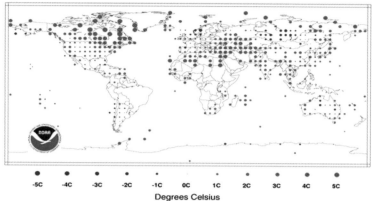

Temperature Anomalies Jan-Dec 2010
(with respect to a 1961-1990 base period)
National Climatic Data Center/NESDIS/NOAA

Figure 1.1. Temperature Anomalies in 2010

it 'polarised' hardly does justice to the degree of extreme feelings climate change can at times provoke. Even the websites of mainstream, serious newspapers such as the *Daily Telegraph* in the UK at times bubble and boil with vitriolic climate scepticism.

The Conservative Party energy minister in the British government, Greg Barker, is not alone in commenting on the strange nature of this polarisation. 'If you look at the extremes of the climate change debate, whether it is the extreme climate sceptics or the extreme climate zealots,' he said, 'there is a slight religiosity there which is weird.'[6]

A high number of prominent climate sceptics – some at the quasi-religious or extreme end but many not – are based in the United States. A climate scepticism conference organised by the Heartland Institute in Washington on 30 June 2011 was described by the *New York Times* correspondent there as having 'the air of a victory lap', in part because of the role that sceptics had played in changing the political landscape in the past two years.[7] Cap-and-trade legislation had been successfully stymied by Republican opposition in the US Congress, which in part draws support from members of the Tea Party, itself closely linked to commentators on Fox News who reflect, energise, and endorse the Tea Party ideology that climate science is something akin to a socialist conspiracy.

The previously held conventional wisdom amongst many senior members of the Republican Party that man-made global warming was taking place has been rapidly abandoned in part to accommodate Tea Party views. Newt Gingrich, who used to support cap-and-trade, described climate change as the 'newest excuse to take control of our lives by left-wing intellectuals'. Rush Limbaugh of Fox News, who believes

---

[6] Nicolas Watt, 'Climate Change Arguments Incite "Weird Religiosity", Says Greg Barker', *Guardian*, 29 June 2011.
[7] Jean Chemnick, 'Scientists Tout Climate Scepticism at Heartland Conference Kickoff', *New York Times*, 30 June 2011.

global warming is 'one of the most preposterous hoaxes in the history of the planet', declared 'bye-bye' to Mitt Romney's prospects as a presidential candidate on hearing that he still believed in man-made global warming. Another candidate who initially campaigned for the Republican Party nomination was Tim Pawlenty. During the campaigning, he disavowed publicly his belief in man-made global warming, saying of his past: 'It was a mistake. It was stupid. It was wrong.'[8]

In many ways, climate change in the USA is an example of 'American exceptionalism'. As a writer for the *New Yorker* has expressed it, the Republican Party is 'stampeding toward an absolutist rejection of climate science that appears unmatched among major political parties around the globe'.[9] But there are also vocal climate sceptics amongst politicians in Canada, and particularly at the fringes of both main parties in Australia where the polarisation has turned particularly unsavoury. In June 2011 the country's leading climate change scientists said they were receiving a stream of abusive emails threatening violence, sexual assault, public smear campaigns, and attacks on family members.[10] The Australian National University moved some of its high-profile scientists into more secure buildings. Professor David Karoly of the University of Melbourne's School of Earth Science told the ABC that he received threats whenever he was interviewed by the media.[11] Some particularly strident commercial radio show presenters were accused of helping to foment – intentionally or not – a climate of extreme antipathy towards the scientists. *The Australian* reported on 16 July what happened to Professor Schellnhuber, the director of the Potsdam Institute for Climate Impact Research, who was opening a climate conference in Melbourne. 'I was confronted with a death threat when I gave my public lecture,' Professor Schellnhuber said. 'Somebody got to his feet and showed me a rope with a noose. He showed me this hangman's rope and he said: "Mr Schellnhuber, welcome to Australia".'[12]

But such polarisation around climate change seems to be largely absent from the politics, public discourse, and media in many other countries. As we shall see, for a whole series of interesting reasons, climate scepticism is seldom seen or heard in the media in newly emerging power houses like Brazil, China, and India. In France climate scepticism is present, particularly through the media presence of the former Socialist minister, Claude Allègre, but in general it is thinner on the ground. The media coverage of climate change in these countries seems to be the polar opposite of that found in parts of the media in the USA, the UK, and Australia. Indeed, in the same week the US media were reporting on the climate scepticism conference and the Australian media on the threats to

---

[8] 'GOP Presidential Hopefuls Dance around Climate Change', *Christian Science Monitor*, 19 June 2011.
[9] Elizabeth Kolbert, 'Storms Brewing', *New Yorker*, 13 June 2011.
[10] Climate sceptics say they have also been subject to hate campaigns. See e.g. the quotes from Professor Timothy Ball in 'Scientists Threatened for "Climate Denial"', *Daily Telegraph*, 11 Mar. 2007.
[11] Oliver Milman, 'Australian Climate Scientists Receive Death Threats', *Guardian*, 6 June 2011.
[12] Brendan Nicholson and Lauren Wilson, 'Climate Anger Dangerous, Says German Physicist', *The Australian*, 16 July 2011.

climate scientists, the *Estado* newspaper in Brazil was highlighting a study that suggested that China's coal burning had created sulphur emissions which had dampened down the rate of global warming.[13] The *Times of India* reported on new research warning that the warming of the ocean's subsurface layer could melt portions of Greenland's underwater ice sheets faster than previously thought.[14] And China's *People's Daily* was headlining its government's call to developed countries to take the lead in adopting verifiable cuts in carbon emissions.[15]

But even within the print media in the same country there can be significant variations as to how much space individual newspapers give to sceptical voices and climate scepticism in general, or indeed how differently papers at times frame their reporting on the same findings from a piece of new research. For example, the article on the emissions from China's coal-burning reported in Brazil's *Estado* was based on a study published in the Proceedings of the National Academy of Sciences on 6 July. It prompted the headline in the climate sceptic *Daily Express* in the UK of 'So much for global warming as planet earth gets colder'. This contrasted with the *Independent*'s 'China's Coal Use Cooled Global Warming' and 'Sulphur from Chinese Power Stations "Masking" Climate Change' favoured by the *Guardian*.[16]

So the issue – and the science – of climate change has become contested, polarised, and politicised – at least in the Anglo-Saxon world. The hugely significant role that the media play in this process has come under intense scrutiny. On the one hand, sceptics frequently attack what they call the 'liberal consensus' found in the BBC and other media outlets for overzealously following the mainstream scientific view and not allowing enough space to points of view that oppose them. On the other, the media are often criticised by the scientists who give weight to the evidence for global warming. They put forward three linked but discrete arguments:

(1) by giving (disproportionate or any) space to sceptics, parts of the media are aiding the process of denial of human-caused global warming amongst politicians and the public;[17]

(2) if they are not actually aiding denial, parts of the media are contributing to public confusion; and

---

[13] *Estado*, 4 July 2011; http://www.estadao.com.br/noticias/vidae,poluicao-do-ar-freia-aquecimento-global,740587,0.htm.
[14] 'Warming Ocean Layers Melt Polar Ice Sheets Faster', *Times of India*, 4 July 2011, http://articles.timesofindia.indiatimes.com/2011-07-04/global-warming/29735612_1_global-warming-ice-sheets-ice-cube.
[15] *People's Daily*, 6 July 2011: http://english.peopledaily.com.cn/90001/90776/90883/7430519.html.
[16] www.express.co.uk/posts/view/256855/So-much-for-global-warming-as-Planet-Earth-gets-colder; www.independent.co.uk/environment/climate-change/chinarsquos-power-stations-generate-lsquofuture-spikersquo-in-global-warming-2306976.html; www.guardian.co.uk/environment/2011/jul/04/sulphur-pollution-china-coal-climate.
[17] Some critics suggest that one of the reasons why some media give too much space to sceptics is because they are too open to the influence or lobbying of climate sceptic groups financed by wealthy individuals or corporate interests. This topic is discussed in Ch. 2.

(3) they are helping to create a climate of doubt which is one of the many obstacles to more robust government action to cut emissions.

None of these three arguments is particularly new. Parts of the media have long been accused of being excessively drawn to controversy and argument in the name of balanced reporting, which can, the critics say, amount to a form of bias. The seminal piece of research on this is a study by the Boykoff brothers in 2004 which concluded that 53% of the articles in four US prestige newspapers between 1998 and 2002 gave equal coverage to views that global warming was due to humans or was natural. This was famously described as 'balance as bias', given the overwhelming scientific consensus (usually described as being over 95%) of climate scientists who accept the evidence for the former.[18]

The 'false balance' debate is still a vigorous one. For example, a February 2010 report from Fairness and Accuracy in Reporting (FAIR) in the USA criticised the mainstream media there for returning to 'the bad old days of false balance'.[19] Also in 2010 the BBC's governing body, the BBC Trust, launched an independent review of its science coverage by genetics professor Steve Jones which among other things was intended to assess the accuracy and impartiality of its reporting of global warming. This was prompted in part by concerns from the sceptics in the audience that their voices were not being heard enough, and from the anti-sceptics that they were being heard too much. In his report released in July 2011, the BBC was generally praised for its science coverage, but amongst Professor Jones's conclusions was his criticism that the BBC was still giving space to the sceptics 'to make statements that are not supported by the facts'.[20]

The former US vice-president Al Gore, a prominent proponent of the case that humans are causing global warming, is in no doubt that parts of the US media still play, in his view, a hugely unhelpful role in promoting the views of sceptics. In June 2011 he described local newspapers and television stations as being 'frightened of the reaction they get from the deniers when they report the science objectively'.[21] He called on supporters

> to let them know that deniers are not the only ones in town with game. It's true that that some media outlets are getting instructions from their owners on this issue, and that others are influenced by big advertisers, but many of them are

[18] M. Boykoff and J. Boykoff, 'Balance as Bias: Global Warming and the US Prestige Press', *Global Environmental Change*, 15/4 (2004): 125–36. As we will see in Ch. 3, Max Boykoff's subsequent research of the US and UK prestige print media suggested that this situation had changed to become more representative of the scientific consensus.

[19] Julie Hollar, '"Climategate" Overshadows Copenhagen: Media Regress to the Bad Old Days of False Balance', *FAIR*, Feb. 2010: www.fair.org/index.php?page=4006.

[20] The report is available at www.bbc.co.uk/bbctrust/assets/files/pdf/our_work/science_impartiality/science_impartiality.pdf.

[21] Al Gore, 'Climate of Denial', *Rolling Stone*, 22 June 2011. His stance was criticised in an article by John Wihbey in the Yale Climate Medium Forum. See www.yaleclimatemediaforum.org/2011/08/al-gore-in-rolling-stone-mocks-the-media/#more-8389.

surprisingly responsive to a genuine outpouring of opinion from their viewers and readers. It is way past time for the ref to do his job.

The debate is equally intense in Australia. A group of prominent climate scientists issued a statement in July 2011 on the state of the science, which included a blistering attack on the media. In it they spoke of 'systemic media failures [which] arise from several presumptions about the way science works, which range from being utterly false to dangerously ill-informed to overtly malicious and mendacious'.[22] According to them, the 'false' was

the presumption of the media ... that scientific opinions must somehow be balanced by an opposing view. While balance is an appropriate conversational frame for the political sphere, it is wholly inappropriate for scientific issues, where what matters is the balance of evidence, not opinion.

After a scathing criticism of the media owned by Rupert Murdoch's Newscorp in Australia, they concluded that, because of the 'phoney debate', 'the Australian media has tragically and thoroughly failed the Australian public'.

Some academic studies suggest that journalistic norms of coverage may have contributed to the lack of public understanding of climate change, and in particular their grasp of where there is scientific consensus and where there is not.[23] Opinion surveys in the USA and the UK regularly indicate for example that the public are confused about what proportion of climate scientists think human-caused global warming is happening. According to the May 2011 survey carried out by the George Mason University on Americans' Global Warming Beliefs and Attitudes, 'only 15 percent correctly understand that the great majority of climate scientists think that global warming is caused mostly by human activities, while 32 percent say they don't know'. In 2008, an Ipsos-MORI poll in the UK found that 60% of respondents agreed with the statement that 'many scientific experts still question if humans are contributing to climate change'.[24]

As Mike Hulme's book *Why we Disagree about Climate Change* eloquently lays out, all sorts of influences and values – cultural, religious, political amongst them – come to bear on an individual's views on global warming, sceptical or otherwise, with more force than an understanding of the science.[25] But the influence of information or

---

[22] Quoted on *Climate Progress* website, 5 July 2011.
[23] See e.g. Catherine Butler and Nick Pidgeon, 'Media Communications and Public Understanding of Climate Change', in Tammy Boyce and Justin Lewis (eds), *Climate Change and the Media* (2009), 47.
[24] Quoted in Robert E.T. Ward, 'Climate Change, the Public, and the Media in the UK', ibid. 60. However, a poll carried out by Cardiff University in early 2010 showed that only 21% of those asked disagreed with the statement that 'most scientists agree humans are causing climate change'. See http://psych.cf.ac.uk/understandingrisk/docs/final_report.pdf, p. 18.
[25] Mike Hulme, *Why we Disagree about Climate Change* (2009), ch. 7.

messages coming from the media is clearly one of them. One recent poll suggested that 60% of those who watch Fox News almost daily 'believe that most scientists do not agree that climate change is occurring, whereas only 30% who never watch it believe that. Only 25% of those who watch CNN almost daily hold that erroneous belief – and only 14% who listen to NPR or PBS almost daily.'[26]

Clearly, part of the reason why Fox News viewers or NPR listeners may be selecting a different broadcaster is to have their views confirmed. But the key point here is that parts of the media stand accused of not distinguishing enough between where there is overwhelming scientific consensus (for example, on the human drivers of global warming), and where there are more legitimate grounds for debate (for example, what are the likely impacts and when are they likely to take place, or what are the best policies for tackling GHG emissions). As Haydn Washington and John Cook argue in their book *Climate Change Denial*, 'climate scientists are very certain about some things, such as the basics of climate change, but less certain about other things … The poorly understood aspects of climate change do *not* invalidate the very well understood parts.'[27] The public, the critics say, is often left with the view there is a great 'climate change debate' taking place on every issue. The point is emphasised by Max Boykoff in a 2011 article about 'outlier views' on climate change. He writes that one of the key challenges facing the mass media is that 'media representations have often collapsed … viewpoints, interventions, and perspectives, largely into the broad brush term of 'climate scepticism'.[28]

The final accusation is that the media's treatment of the issue contributes to the lack of government action on tackling climate change. The argument, simply expressed, is that if significant numbers of the general public are sceptical – maybe as many as 20–40% in the developed world – or at least are confused or downplay it, then this can stand in the way of robust measures.[29] In their award-winning book, *The Merchants of Doubt*, Naomi Oreskes and Erik Conway write that in the USA 'this divergence between the state of the science and how it was presented in the major media helped make it easy for our government to do nothing about global warming'.[30]

All these debates became more intense in the aftermath of the 'Climategate' affair and the questioning of parts of the reports by the Intergovernmental Panel on Climate Change (IPCC) which emerged at the end of 2009 and ran through some of the world's media through 2010. Details of the two controversies have been widely documented

[26] World Public Opinion, 'Misinformation and the 2010 Election: A Study of the US Electorate', 10 Dec. 2010, p. 23: www.worldpublicopinion.org/pipa/pdf/dec10/Misinformation_Dec10_rpt.pdf.

[27] Haydn Washington and John Cook, *Climate Change Denial: Heads in the Sand* (2011), 7.

[28] Max Boykoff, 'Public Enemy No. 1? Understanding Media Representations of Outlier Views on Climate Change', *American Behavioral Scientist* (2011), 5.

[29] See e.g. Joe Smith blog, 26 May 2011. https://citizenjoesmith.wordpress.com/.

[30] Naomi Oreskes and Erik Conway, The Merchants of Doubt: *How a Handful of Scientists Obscured the Truth on Issues from Tobacco Smoke to Global Warming* (2010), 215.

and analysed.[31] (See Appendix 1 for a brief overview of 'Climategate'.) In the former, scientists at the climatic research unit at the University of East Anglia in the UK were cleared by official inquiries of accusations that they had manipulated results and kept critics out of science publications, but were found to be 'unhelpful and defensive' in response to 'reasonable requests for information'. The inquiries also concluded that the basic science of climate change had not been undermined. The IPCC was subject to intense criticism in the UK and US media on several fronts, but in particular for the inclusion of a mistaken prediction that the Himalayan glaciers could disappear by 2035, a controversy often known as 'Himalayagate'.

As we shall see, there are many different types of climate sceptics. But several of them were widely quoted in the UK and US media's coverage of both 'Climategate' and the IPCC controversies. Some, like Benny Peiser of the Global Warming Policy Foundation (GWPF) in the UK, argued that this was to be welcomed as an essential corrective to the unquestioning attitude of much of the media's sometimes over-reverent treatment of climate scientists and the IPCC. Peiser wrote that 'for far too long, scientific organisations and the mainstream media did not give appropriate space to authoritative critics of inflated climate alarm'. Others maintained that the ways in which climate sceptics were reported and in particular the amount of space they were being given was disproportionate to their importance. Typical was Robin McKie, science editor at the *Observer* who argued that

> *only a handful of truly reputable scientists are sceptical about the link between global warming and our industrial activities. More to the point, that minority is given a vastly disproportionate amount of publicity. Note the same old faces – the Lawsons and Moncktons – who are trotted out to speak on* Newsnight *or* Channel 4 News *whenever climate change is debated.*[32]

This study has been prompted by these important debates but is largely agnostic about them. It is not its purpose to criticise climate sceptics. There are plenty of NGOs, politicians, scientists, academics, and polemicists who do that and no shortage of articulate sceptics who can defend their positions and right to be heard. Nor is its purpose to criticise journalists, editors, or proprietors for giving not enough or too much space and airtime to their voices – again, there are plenty of others who do that. Rather, our purpose was to map the rise in the prevalence of climate-sceptic voices in the print media in a variety of countries in late 2009/10, and try to explain the differences within and between them and the drivers behind them.

[31] See e.g. Fred Pearce, *The Climate Files* (2010), and Myanna Lahsen, 'Climategate: The Role of the Social Sciences and the Vulnerability of the Strong Front Strategy', unpublished manuscript.
[32] Robin McKie v Benny Peiser, *Observer*, 7 Feb. 2010: www.guardian.co.uk/commentisfree/2010/feb/07/robin-mckie-benny-peiser-climate.

Part of the impetus for this came from previous research done by the RISJ which strongly suggested that climate scepticism was a common phenomenon in the media of the Anglo-Saxon world but not elsewhere. In our study of the reporting of climate science during the 2009 UN Copenhagen summit, individual climate sceptics were not quoted at all in the print media in the countries of the global south we surveyed.[33] Newspapers of widely divergent ideologies, readership profiles, and formats in large parts of Asia (including China and India), Latin America, and Africa seem hardly to mention climate sceptics, or when they do, they rely on international agencies quoting UK or US sources.

If climate scepticism in the media is largely an Anglo-Saxon phenomenon, why is that so? What accounts for these differences – journalistic culture and norms or wider societal factors like the strength of organised lobby groups, sceptical political parties, or more direct in-country experience of the impacts of the changing climate? Why is it that climate science has become much more politicised in some countries than in others? Does the political perspective of a newspaper or proprietor drive the coverage? Why do left-wing or liberal newspapers seldom follow a sceptical editorial line? What role is played by the recent expansion of journalism of opinion or 'attitude' (rather than record) with strong, ideologically driven commentary and discussion, particularly in the tabloids in the UK and Fox News in the USA? As the business models of newspapers come under threat from the Web, how significant is the wider issue of declining budgets and specialism, particularly in the US print media? All sorts of factors impinge on, or drive, a particular newspaper's coverage of climate change, but in different countries and media environments, some factors are clearly more influential than others.

The following chapters aim both to document the presence or absence of sceptical voices in the print media in various countries, but also to try to give tentative answers to some of these questions. Chapter 2 gives a general introduction to the different types of climate scepticism, describing how even the term is contested, but also laying out the various ways authors have tried to capture the full spectrum of sceptics who exist. Four examples of prominent, but very different, climate sceptics are given. It then examines some of the particular features of American society and politics which make the phenomenon particularly prevalent there in contrast to many other countries. It describes the close nexus between climate scepticism and a particular brand of conservative ideology embodied in the Tea Party, suggesting that at times scepticism can be driven more by political ideology than by scientific inquiry. The chapter also describes four features of American 'exceptionalism', including the power of lobbying groups, which are not replicated in other countries.

---

[33] This was largely due to the fact that the coverage of 'Climategate', where most sceptics would be expected to be quoted, was concentrated mainly in developed countries, primarily the UK and the USA. Only 20% of the coverage on 'Climategate' originated in developing countries. See James Painter, *Summoned by Science: Reporting Climate Change at Copenhagen and Beyond* (2010), 51.

Chapter 3 gives an overview of academic studies and other research on the portrayal of mainstream climate science in the media of various countries of the world, and of the prevalence or absence of sceptical voices. There have been few studies specifically on the prevalence of sceptical voices in the media, but research on the more general issue of 'false balance' would strongly suggest that the questioning of mainstream science is more of an Anglo-Saxon phenomenon, and is particularly prevalent in parts of the media in the USA, Australia, Canada, and the UK. Within the global south and continental Europe, there does seem to be a general trend of the media not offering as much space to sceptic voices as in parts of the Anglo-Saxon press. Brief mention is also made of how 'Climategate' changed the perception of some journalists in the Western world about the climate change story, at least in the immediate months that followed it.

Chapter 4 contains the meat of the research findings from the comparison of the print media's treatment of climate sceptical voices. Apart from looking at any increase in the amount of space given to sceptics and significant country variations, we also asked whether there were important differences between left-leaning and right-leaning newspapers, in which part of the newspaper were sceptical voices most likely to be found, which types of sceptical voices were most included, and what was the background – professional or otherwise – of the sceptics who were quoted. The results were based on content analysis of two samples of the print media in six countries (Brazil, China, France, India, the UK, and the USA) over two three-month periods in 2007 and 2009/10. In most cases, examples of a left-leaning and of a right-leaning or centrist newspaper were chosen for the analysis. The methodology, its limitations, and the main results are laid out and then discussed here and in Appendix 3.

Chapter 5 includes country-specific discussions of the results from Brazil, China, France, India, and the USA. Semi-structured interviews with journalists and editors from most (but not all) of the newspapers included in the study are supplemented by interviews with academics or experts in those countries' media to give some context and some explanation for the results. In each country, possible factors explaining the presence or absence of sceptical voices are explored.

Chapter 6 gives the results from similar content analysis for the same periods from all ten major UK national newspapers. We expanded the UK sample in order to get a better sense of any divergences between broadsheet and tabloid coverage, or more importantly, to have a larger selection of right- and left-leaning newspapers to track any differences in the reporting. Again, interviews with journalists and editors from most of the ten newspapers included were used to help give a brief interpretation of the results. Finally in Chapter 7 we present the conclusions, some final thoughts, and some issues for journalists to consider.

2. The Nature of Climate Scepticism

The language of scepticism

Even the word 'sceptic' is contested. Mainstream climate scientists and those who question the science both want to hold onto, or seize, the word as their own. Emily Shuckburgh is a scientist at the British Antarctic Survey, whom the *Financial Times* describes as being in the vanguard of a new generation fighting back against those who reject mainstream science. She pointed out to the paper that 'scepticism is a major part of science, and it's a shame it has been appropriated. That leads to a lot of confusion. If we could reclaim the word ... that would be progress.'[34]

Dr Shuckburgh is not the first scientist to make the point. It is a view echoed by a top climate scientist at Oxford University who was quoted by Lord Krebs in an opinion piece in the London *Times* saying that 'It's odd that people talk about "climate sceptics" as though they are a special category. All of us in the climate science community are climate sceptics. It's our job to question and challenge everything.'[35] As Professor Krebs described it, 'any scientist will tell you that when you turn up at a conference, the audience will do its best to tear your findings to pieces: no one takes anything for granted'.

Part of the problem is that the word 'sceptic' is not free of value. To be sceptical is almost always a good thing, in the way that good journalists are often taught to be sceptical rather than cynical about issues they are reporting on. The opposite of being sceptical can be to be gullible, which is not a common aspiration. For a scientist, scepticism is a proper and necessary part of scientific inquiry.

In the view of many mainstream climate scientists, climate change sceptics want to be called sceptics when they are really 'deniers'. In other words, they are accused of not accepting the overwhelming weight of the evidence, which is not scepticism but denial. An analysis of the difference between scepticism and denial is contained in an article by Michael Shermer, an adjunct professor at Claremont Graduate University in

---

[34] Andrew Jack, 'Battle Lines', *Financial Times*, 24 June 2011.
[35] John Krebs, 'We might Err, But Science is Self-Correcting', *The Times*, 8 Feb. 2010.

California, who wrote in a special edition of *New Scientist* called the 'Age of Denial' that, whereas scepticism is integral to the scientific process, denial 'is the automatic gainsaying of a claim regardless of the evidence for it. [It] is typically driven by ideology or religious belief, where the commitment to the belief takes precedence over the evidence.'[36] Shermer suggests that a practical way of telling the difference is the extent to which they are willing to update their positions in response to new information. 'Sceptics change their minds. Deniers just keep on denying.'

Some argue therefore that it is more accurate to call some climate sceptics 'deniers' or even 'denialists', whilst others prefer 'contrarians' or 'outliers'. The argument against calling them 'deniers' is that it seems rather a Stalinist term, and that it has echoes of those who deny the Holocaust. In other words, it is almost a term of abuse. As a columnist in the *Sunday Express* pointed out, 'What we are dealing with here is not science but a new form of religion. Those of us who question its scriptures are called "deniers", an innuendo designed to link us to the Holocaust. Heretics are to be punished.'[37] It is not just right-wing commentators who object. James Randerson, an environment editor at the *Guardian*, also dislikes the term, as 'making the link with the 20th century's most colossal work of industrial-scale evil – the Holocaust – plays into the hands of those who want to convince the waverers that this is purely a political argument.'[38]

A more significant problem is that many people labelled 'sceptics' are not in fact deniers. Often they don't deny that global warming is happening or that it is essentially human-caused. Rather, they are sceptical about whether human-driven warming is dangerous or catastrophic, or whether it requires large-scale policies to tackle it. They can argue any one or combination of the following: that climate models are essentially flawed or inaccurate and/or it is not known with enough certainty what the impacts will be; that urgent action by governments and/or substantial government spending on all or some aspects of mitigation or adaptation to counter global warming is not necessary (for example, short-term costs are too high, some parts of the world could benefit, the response is disproportionate to the threat, the impacts are too uncertain, and so on). Some observers have labelled some of these types of sceptics as the 'non-denier deniers'.[39]

To anyone grappling with the nomenclature, it rapidly becomes apparent that the variety of sceptics is so wide that any single label is hugely problematic. Different authors have come up with a wide range of definitions and typologies. For example, Stefan Rahmstorf, a mainstream German scientist at the Potsdam Institute, argues that 'sceptics' essentially come in three types: Trend sceptics (those who

---

[36] Michael Shermer, 'I am a Sceptic, But I'm Not a Denier', *New Scientist*, 15 May 2010.
[37] Neil Hamilton, 'The Great Global Warming Con', *Sunday Express*, 29 Nov. 2009.
[38] James Randerson, 'Christopher Booker's Wilful Climate Change Ignorance Gathers Pace', 25 Feb.: www.guardian.co.uk/environment/blog/2009/feb/25/climate-change-denial-christopher-booker.
[39] James Hoggan, *Climate Cover-Up: The Crusade to Deny Global Warming* (2009), as quoted in Washington and Cook, *Climate Change Denial*, 78.

deny the warming trend), Attribution sceptics (those who accept the trend and attribute it to natural causes), and Impacts sceptics (those who accept human causation of the warming trend but claim the impacts will be beneficial or benign).[40] The academic Peter Jacques and colleagues have divided the more general type of 'environmental scepticism' into four key themes: those who (1) deny the seriousness of environmental problems and dismiss scientific evidence documenting them, (2) question the importance and wisdom of regulatory policies to address them, (3) endorse an anti-regulatory/anti-corporate liability position, and (4) consider environmental protection to threaten Western progress.[41]

The term 'contrarian' is often favoured by media academics in the United States. Some scholars there, like sociologist Aaron McCright, have defined it more in relation to the loudness of the sceptics' position or the provenance of their funding as those who 'vocally challenge what they see as a false consensus of "mainstream climate science" ... by criticizing mainstream climate science in general and pre-eminent climate scientists, often with substantial financial support from fossil fuels industry organizations and conservative think tanks'.[42] 'Deniers' have also been given various taxonomies of their own. While sociologist Professor Kari Norgaard describes three types of denial as literal ('it's just not happening'), interpretative ('it's happening, but human beings aren't causing it'), and implicatory (acting as if something does not matter), the biologist Peter Doherty has gone for outright deniers, combative confrontationalists, professional 'controversialists', and conflicted 'naysayers'. The mathematician Ian Enting has distinguished them by the ways he says they distort the scientific evidence by 'outright lies', 'twisting phrasing', and 'removing qualifiers'.[43]

This last categorisation leads into a typology of the most commonly aired – but very different – *arguments* used by sceptics. There is not space here to go through them, but several authors have done so.[44] In contrast to the various types of sceptics stand the 'mainstream' scientists. The Brazil-based author and academic, Myanna Lahsen, defines them as those who:

(1) work in official scientific institutions, mainly accredited universities and federal research laboratories,

(2) publish primarily, if not exclusively, in scientific, peer-reviewed journals, and

[40] Quoted in Washington and Cook, *Climate Change Denial*, 11.
[41] P. J. Jacques, R. E. Dunlap, and M. Freeman, 'The Organization of Denial', *Environmental Politics*, 17 (2008), 349–85.
[42] Aaron McCright, 'Dealing with Climate Change Contrarians', in Susanne Moser and Lisa Dilling (eds), *Creating a Climate for Change* (Cambridge: CUP, 2007), 201.
[43] Kari Norgaard, *Living in Denial: Climate Change, Emotions and Everyday Life* (Boston, MA: MIT Press, 2011). Doherty and Enting are described in Washington and Cook, Climate Change Denial, 11.
[44] See e.g. Washington and Cook, *Climate Change Denial*, ch. 3.

(3) do not have extensive material and discursive ties to the vested interests and conservative think tanks that propel the anti-environmental movement, [and] in particular a strong, explicit aversion to government regulation.[45]

However, many observers would say that we also need a typology of the 'mainstream' scientists, to separate the 'radicals' or 'alarmists' like James Hansen, Stewart Brand, and James Lovelock, who warn repeatedly that the human production of GHGs is pushing the planet to relatively imminent disaster, to less apocalyptic voices often associated with the more conservative and consensual reports of the IPCC.[46]

Discussion about the typology of scepticism has generated such a large amount of analysis by climate scientists, sociologists, and media academics that a cynic would say we need a new typology of typologies. It is not the purpose of this study to enter into a lengthy discussion of the merits of any particular typology. However, in our view, it does seem helpful to be aware of how scholars and others distinguish between scepticism, contrarianism, and denialism in the following ways. The term 'contrarians' as described above does capture the way some are very vocal and heavily involved in the policy debate, sometimes as a result of their close ties to vested economic interests. 'Denialism' can help to distinguish those who really do not think that the world temperatures are warming up, or more likely that the anthropogenic contribution (burning fossil fuels) to global warming is overstated, negligible, or non-existent compared to other factors like natural variations or sun spots. As argued above, 'sceptics' can and do question much about possible shortcomings in climate data and the models, or are wary of any bandwagon of consensus science, or are unconvinced that urgent, robust action is needed. It may be that denialists use the arguments of sceptics to disguise their denialism, but there is no doubt they are very different.

For the purposes of this study, we run the risk of being accused of being lazy as we have opted for the journalistic shorthand of 'sceptics' while recognising the differences and problems with the term. After all, this is how they are most commonly known amongst the public and media alike. We have tried to capture the main differences between the sceptics in the coding used in the content analysis of the 20 newspapers included in this study. (See Chapter 4 and the appendices for the discussion.) This is because for journalists and the public alike it is helpful to have these distinctions constantly in mind. As we said in Chapter 1, some areas of the climate change debate seem to be more legitimate than others, and we shall return to this point in our conclusions.

---

[45] Myanna Lahsen, 'Climategate', 3. Lahsen adds that they also 'tend to believe that the global climate has warmed and that human action may be one of the causes'.
[46] Lumping together all 'radicals' is also problematic. James Hansen is different e.g. to Brand and Lovelock in that he regularly publishes peer-reviewed papers on climate science.

Four examples of sceptics

The following short descriptions of four prominent sceptics who receive a good deal of press coverage illustrate just how multifaceted scepticism and sceptics can be in terms of (a) what they are sceptical about, (b) their links (or not) to lobby groups, fossil fuel funding, or universities, (c) their presence on the internet, and (d) their degree of scientific credibility.

Some of the most prominent sceptics who are based in the USA but quoted in other Anglophone media have been shown to receive funding from fossil fuel companies. A prominent example is Dr Patrick Michaels, who was a research professor in environmental science at the University of Virginia for 30 years, and is currently a senior research fellow at the George Mason University. He has an academic background in climatology, and does not contend the basic science of global warming but argues the impacts will be minor or even beneficial. His links to the fossil fuel industry are particularly controversial. In an interview with CNN in August 2010 he said that 'about 40 per cent' of his funding came from oil industry sources.[47] The statement prompted a letter from the Democrat Congressman Henry Waxman to the chair of the US House Energy and Commerce Committee in January 2011 asking for clarification about the amount of industry funding Michaels received, as he had previously told the Committee in February 2009 that a much lower figure – about 3% – of his US$4.2m in financial support came from the oil and gas industry.[48]

Michaels is also a senior fellow of the Cato Institute which has received funding from ExxonMobil and Koch Industries. He has a high media profile in the USA. For example, he was quoted in the *New York Times* and the *Wall Street Journal* and appeared on CNN in the weeks after 'Climategate' broke.[49] He was also quoted seven times in five different UK newspapers during the 2009/10 period of our study, and was one of the sceptics who most frequently appeared. The reason why he is an interesting case study for media analysts is partly because his links to industry funding are not always mentioned. For example, researchers at FAIR (Fairness and Accuracy in Reporting) in the USA found that in December 2009, he appeared on CNN five times, Fox News once, and NBC once, and the links were not mentioned in any of them.[50] In our study of the UK media, some of the newspapers (the left-leaning *Guardian* and *Independent*) usually mentioned his funding sources, whilst others (the right-leaning *Daily Express*, the *Daily Telegraph*, and the *Sunday Times*) did not. The *Express* described him as 'Professor Patrick Michaels, an environmentalist from the Cato Institute', the *Telegraph* as 'Dr Michaels, tracked down by this newspaper

[47] For a transcript and a clip of the CNN interview, see www.desmogblog.com/climate-skeptic-pat-michaels-admits-cnn-forty-percent-his-funding-comes-oil-industry.
[48] For a copy of the Waxman letter, see http://democrats.energycommerce.house.gov/index.php?q=news/waxman-asks-upton-to-examine-dr-patrick-michaels-s-testimony; for more background see Suzanne Goldenberg, 'Climate Sceptic "Misled Congress over Funding from Oil Industry"', *Guardian*, 25 Jan. 2011.
[49] Kate Sheppard, 'Climategate: What Really Happened?', *Mother Jones*, 21 Apr. 2011, p. 13.
[50] Julie Hollar, 'Climategate Overshadows Copenhagen', 4.

to the Cato Institute in Washington D.C., and the *Sunday Times* as a 'prominent climate sceptic'.[51] Andy Revkin of the *New York Times* says he understands how lack of space, expertise, and time may mean short cuts by journalists, but 'it is irresponsible not to say who he works for'.[52]

The main reason why it is worth highlighting the case of Patrick Michaels is that it is illustrative of one type of climate sceptic often appearing in the media on both sides of the Atlantic who has strong links both with fossil fuel sources of funding and with a right-wing think tank whose position on climate change is consistent with an ideological opposition to regulation of the market. He is an example of 'organised scepticism'. But other types of sceptic do not have a professional background in climate science, have no known links to fossil fuel industries, and are probably not driven much by ideology. As the journalist Fred Pearce writes in his journalistic account of 'Climategate', probably the key sceptic player behind the affair, the Canadian Steve McIntyre, and others like him are more like highly motivated 'amateurs' (in the sense they are not scientists linked to universities). Pearce writes that, despite McIntyre's background in commercial mining, there is no evidence yet to emerge which supports the view that he was funded by commercial concerns. As Pearce describes it, there is 'a new breed of critic without overt political or commercial motivation, amateur scientific sleuths driven more by curiosity and healthy scepticism for received wisdom'.[53]

Steve McIntyre and others working with him wanted access to climate data so they could test for themselves the conclusions reached by mainstream climate scientists. He is a trained mathematician, who is probably more driven by his passion for data than ideology. According to one US magazine, 'he believes that the planet is warming and humans are playing a role, but [doesn't] think this is as much as a problem as it has been made out'.[54] He has been invited to speak at briefings organised by the Marshall Institute and the Competitive Enterprise Institute, but has said that he does not oppose government regulations on principle, which marks him off from such lobby groups. What is more significant from a media perspective is that McIntyre's public profile is intimately linked to his website, ClimateAudit, where his tone is regarded by some as more polemical than in his public appearances.[55] Andy Revkin of the *New York Times* agrees that there is

> *a new breed of sceptics, although it's part of what has long been a spectrum of feelings about climate change. There*

---

[51] The references are to *Express*, 17 Dec. 2009, *Telegraph*, 28 Nov. 2009, and *The Sunday Times*, 29 Nov. 2009. In the *Independent*, Michaels was labelled in a column piece on 24 Dec. 2009 as a 'dissenting scientist' but eight days earlier an article in the same newspaper described him as having received US$100,000 from energy companies. Likewise, two of the three mentions in the *Guardian* highlighted the link (the articles appeared on 8 Dec. 2009, 2 Feb. 2010, and 4 Feb. 2010).
[52] Author interview, July 2011.
[53] Pearce, *Climate Files*, 12.
[54] Sheppard, 'Climategate: What Really Happened?', 4.
[55] See his posts on http://climateaudit.org; and Sheppard, 'Climategate: What Really Happened?', 3.

are people who are fascinated with puzzles and statistics, and they've served a role. McIntyre has improved how some institutions do their statistics. Whether he'll be seen in the long haul as having had a positive influence on climate science is a question yet to be determined.

In a not dissimilar vein, the prominent sceptic British Lord Christopher Monckton, who is based in the UK but who is well-known in the USA and Australia, has never been accused of being funded by big business, although he is known for his anti-communist ideology.[56] He often denounces the UNFCCC negotiations as an attempt by leftists to impose a new world government intent on restricting individual freedom. He disputes the basic science of climate change but is not known to have published in established science journals. He was invited to give testimony to a US House Subcommittee on Energy and the Environment in March 2009 (which prompted a strong rebuttal by mainstream climate scientists[57]). A BBC TV documentary in January 2011 showed his high profile in the Australian media and considerable appeal to the climate sceptic movement there.[58] His 2009 visit received saturation coverage in the media (see discussion in Chapter 3), but his 2011 visit was shrouded in considerable controversy after he likened the government chief climate adviser, Professor Ross Garnaut, to Hitler, a comparison for which he later apologised.[59] He had previously compared campaigners from NGOs during the Copenhagen summit to the 'Hitler Youth'.[60] He has also run into trouble with the clerk of parliaments in the UK for claiming to be a member of the House of Lords.[61] Monckton is different from McIntyre in that he is affiliated to a political party (he is the leader of the UK Independence Party, or UKIP, in Scotland). In both cases, they may have links to think tanks or lobby groups but their scepticism has much less institutional support.

The final high-profile sceptic we mention is the Dane Bjørn Lomborg, who again is very different from the other three, particularly in what he is sceptical about. He is not a trained climate scientist but has a Ph.D. in political science. He is one of the world's most prominent sceptics, in part because of his high media profile – he writes a regular column for the *Wall Street Journal*, regularly appears in the US media, and was registered as a CNN journalist at the Copenhagen conference in December 2009. He is the author of the best-selling book *The Skeptical Environmentalist* and *Cool It*, which has also been made into a film. He

[56] Greenpeace, *Dealing in Doubt: The Climate Change Denial Industry and Climate Science* (2010), 1.
[57] See the *Climate Progress* website on 21 Sept. 2010.
[58] BBC4, 'Meet the Climate Sceptics', Storyville, 31 Jan. 2011. In his report on the BBC, Professor Steve Jones said the programme made Monckton's isolation from mainstream beliefs very clear. He also described Lord Monckton as 'without doubt, a man who adds to the gaiety of nations and ... a skilled communicator of his views'. See p. 72 of his report: www.bbc.co.uk/bbctrust/assets/files/pdf/our_work/science_impartiality/science_impartiality.pdf.
[59] www.telegraph.co.uk/earth/environment/climatechange/8594194/Outrage-as-Lord-Monckton-calls-Australian-climate-change-adviser-a-Nazi.html.
[60] www.guardian.co.uk/environment/blog/2009/dec/11/monckton-calls-activists-hitler-youth.
[61] www.guardian.co.uk/environment/2011/jul/18/climate-monckton-member-house-lords.

is not sceptical about the basics of climate science, although he disputes some of the mainstream findings about its costs and impacts. He has expressed scepticism about the need for rapid, large-scale investment to tackle climate change, although he seemed to modify this position in 2010.[62] He has argued that it would be better to spend money on higher priorities like poverty eradication, HIV/Aids, or malaria, although critics say these could well get worse as a result of climate change. He has also been embroiled in controversy over the use of data and other scientific methods in his books.[63]

Climate scepticism in the USA

As can be seen, the four sceptics are very different but all of them enjoy a high profile in the USA. This is the country where climate scepticism has particularly strong roots, is well-organised, and better funded. As mentioned in Chapter 1, it is also the country where a sizeable chunk of a mainstream political party, the Republicans, is currently deeply sceptical about global warming. Despite a long tradition of environmentalism from Republican presidents such as Teddy Roosevelt and Richard Nixon, Republicans or conservatives are now more hostile to environmental issues in general. The difference, according to some authors, is the rise in one strand of conservative ideology, with a more free-market and libertarian tint, as exemplified in the Tea Party.[64] A survey published in September 2011 by the Yale and George Mason universities showed that only 34% of Tea Party supporters believed global warming was happening, compared to 53% for Republicans who were not Tea Party supporters, and 78% for Democrats.[65]

The same survey showed that Tea Party supporters have stronger individualistic values than all the other groups, and particularly strong anti-government attitudes. Indeed, global warming has been added to a long list of issues like health care, gun rights, and abortion, which feed 'a new strain of populism … nourished by the same libertarian impulses that have unsettled American society for a half a century'.[66] The proposed way of combating climate change is normally via large government spending and higher taxes, which of course have been deeply resisted for many years by those sectors of American society suspicious of big Federal government.

[62] In an article on 30 Aug. 2010, the *Guardian* described him as 'the world's most high-profile sceptic' and went on to suggest he had performed a U-turn by advocating US$100bn a year needed to fight climate change.
[63] For a full discussion of Bjørn Lomborg, see Hoggan, *Climate Cover-Up*, 118ff.; Washington and Cook, *Climate Change Denial*, ch. 4; Christina Larson and Joshua Keating, 'The FP Guide to Climate Skeptics', *Foreign Policy*, 26 Feb. 2010, and Michael Svoboda, 'A Critical Review of Bjorn Lomborg's Cool It … and of Media "Complicity" in Climate Contrarianism', *Yale Forum on Climate Change and the Media*, 12 May 2011.
[64] See e.g. Geoffrey Heal, 'Environmental Politics', paper presented to 'The Irrational Economist' conference, Wharton School 2008: www.theirrationaleconomist.com/abstracts/Heal_EnvPolitics.pdf.
[65] The survey described them as Tea Party 'members', as the respondents identified themselves as such. See 'Politics and Global Warming: Democrats, Republicans, Independents and the Tea Party', 7 Sept. 2011: www.climatechangecommunication.org/images/files/PoliticsGlobalWarming2011.pdf.
[66] Mark Lilla, 'The Tea Party Jacobins', *New York Review of Books*, 27 May 2010.

A report in *Nature* magazine in July 2011 clearly illustrates this close nexus between libertarianism and climate scepticism in the USA. Joe Bast, the head of the climate sceptic Heartland Institute, told the magazine it was only natural that a libertarian like him would decide to question the scientific foundation for climate change. *Nature* reported that

> *Getting serious about global warming means implementing government regulation, going after industry, raising taxes, interfering in markets – all anathema to a conservative agenda. 'The left has no reason to look under the hood of global warming,' [Bast] says. 'The right does, and that's what happened.'*[67]

Indeed, in the USA the debate about the causes of global warming and what to do about it has become a proxy for a debate about politics – big government versus small government, free markets or government intervention, individual freedom against the power of the establishment. American consumers are used to relatively cheap energy costs so any attempt to increase them is often seen as an unwelcome government intervention. So climate change is frequently viewed through a political and not a scientific lens. Even though Tea Party supporters are the most sceptical within the Republican Party, generally if you are a Republican voter, you are much more likely to doubt the science of climate change than if you are a Democrat voter. In 2011 researchers at Michigan State University published a study which found that by 2010 only 29% of Republican voters saw man-made warming as real, compared to 70% of Democratic voters. The study pointed out that the gap between conservatives and liberals on belief in global warming widened from 18% in 2001 to 44% in 2010.[68] Curtis Brainard, a long-term observer of the media and climate change for the Columbia Journalism Review, summed up the situation in the USA in 2011. 'Those on the left, politicians on the left, and just citizens on the left,' he said, 'almost universally would like to introduce more mainstream measures to address climate change. It's the exact opposite for those on the right. Partisan bias actually increases and the gap widens with higher levels of education on both sides.'[69]

In other Anglo-Saxon countries such as the UK and Australia where climate scepticism has a significant presence, views on climate change are not defined along political lines to the same extent. Nor are the main political parties imbued with same degree of scepticism. In the UK, from 2006 onwards the current prime minister, David Cameron, made

[67] Jeff Tollefson, 'Climate-Change Politics: The Sceptic Meets his Match', *Nature*, 27 July 2011: www.nature.com/news/2011/110727/full/475440a.html.
[68] Aaron M. McCright and Riley E. Dunlap, 'The Politicization of Climate Change and Polarization in the American Public's Views of Global Warming, 2001–2010', *Sociological Quarterly*, 52/2 (2011), 155–94.
[69] Author interview, July 2011.

a conscious effort to realign the Conservative Party with a green agenda, including a concern for global warming. His coalition government promised to be the 'greenest ever'. Despite pressure from the fringes, the main body of the Conservative Party leadership was publicly supportive of mainstream climate science during the period of this study. Climate-sceptic ideology became a minority right-wing view reflected only at the edges of the Conservative Party and in the British National Party and UKIP. In Australia, the leader of the opposition Liberal Party, Tony Abbott, has made many different statements about climate change, and at times seems to question the validity of climate science. But most MPs from the main parties believe in the science of climate change even though they may differ sharply over what policies to adopt to confront it, and in particular the merits of a carbon tax. Outright deniers or contrarians are found on the fringes of the party.

Organised climate scepticism is also very prevalent in the USA. Many sceptical climate scientists, some with links to think tanks and lobby groups, are based there and in Canada, but they have an international reach way beyond their borders. For example, as we shall see in Chapter 6, of the 18 sceptic scientists quoted in the UK media in the periods we analysed, 11 were based in these two North American countries. In recent years strong lobby groups have appeared in other countries like Australia and the UK, but the practice originates in the USA. A review of the academic and journalistic studies of the USA suggests answers to why climate scepticism has its roots there and why it still flourishes.[70]

There would seem to be four key points worth stressing. (i) The historical trajectory of climate scepticism or denialism in the USA is linked to other scientific issues beyond climate science. (ii) Much of the momentum behind climate scepticism comes from US conservative think tanks, some with funding from fossil fuel companies. This more organised type of scepticism includes media campaigns as part of their strategy, which is often designed merely to sow doubt about climate science rather than disprove it. (iii) Much of the most active and combative climate scepticism is found in the USA and Canada on the blogosphere. Some of this is probably strongly motivated by political ideology, but much of it is driven in part by a desire to pick holes in some aspect of the mainstream science. (iv) The exceptional nature of the US political system includes a pervasive lobbying culture not replicated to the same extent in other countries.

Several books and articles have charted the way climate science denial is only the latest popular science-related issue that some American scientists have taken up as a cause.[71] Oreskes and Conway have mapped the way in which starting at the end of the 1970s a small number of scientists, some linked to the conservative George C. Marshall Institute

---

[70] A selection of these is listed in the Bibliography.
[71] Oreskes and Conway, *Merchants of Doubt*, Hoggan, *Climate Cover-Up*, and Riley E. Dunlap and Aaron M. McCright, 'Climate Change Denial: Sources, Actors and Strategies', in *Routledge Handbook of Climate Change and Society* (2010), ch. 14.

in Washington, joined up with US think thanks and private corporations to challenge scientific evidence on a host of contemporary issues. As they write in their introduction,

> *In the early years, much of the money for this effort came from the tobacco industry; in later years, it came from foundations, think tanks, and the fossil fuel industry. They claimed the link between smoking and cancer remained unproven. They insisted that scientists were mistaken about the risks and limitations of SDI (Strategic Defense Initiative). They argued that acid rain was caused by volcanoes, and so was the ozone hole. They charged that the Environmental Protection Agency had rigged the science surrounding secondhand smoke. Most recently – over the course of nearly two decades and against the face of mounting evidence – they dismissed the reality of global warming.*[72]

These authors and others have tracked the central role played by two US physicists, Fred Singer and Fred Seitz, who the researchers say had carried out little original research on any of the issues they spoke loudly about. But the two were able to enjoy the ears of influential politicians and high-ranking military officers, and were frequently quoted in the media. Some authors have argued that a possible explanation of their motivation was an element of professional jealousy, as they felt that their status as physicists was being undermined or usurped in policy-making circles by the more recent focus on environmental science.[73] But the key point is that climate science denial in the USA cannot be seen outside the wider arena of other campaigns against mainstream science, most of which have the policy implication of heavy state investment or regulation to combat a public health risk or environmental pollution.

Some authors have made a convincing case that the growth of American climate science scepticism also has to be seen within the wider promotion of environmental scepticism. As two US sociologists have written, 'since the early 1990s there has been a comprehensive effort to portray environmental science as "junk science", frequently with the assistance of sympathetic "experts" often drawn from academia, and with enormous help from conservative media figures such as right-wing commentator Rush Limbaugh and Fox News'.[74] The same authors found that of the more than 140 books published until 2005 which espoused environmental scepticism (many of which focused on climate change), more than 90% were linked to a conservative think tank in the USA or other nation. All but 20 were published after 1990. Their

---

[72] Oreskes and Conway, *Merchants of Doubt*, 6.
[73] Myanna Lahsen, 'Experiences of Modernity in the Greenhouse: A Cultural Analysis of a Physicist "Trio" Supporting the Conservative Backlash Against Global Warming', *Glob. Environ. Change*, 18 (2008), 204–19, quoted in Washington and Cook, *Climate Change Denial*, 79, and Dunlap and McCright, 'Climate Change Denial', 247.
[74] Dunlap and McCright, 'Climate Change Denial', 244.

studies have also focused on how a limited group of conservative think tanks, including the George C. Marshall Institute, were able to promote successfully the views of a small number of contrarian scientists who received a high degree of media visibility. Several authors argue that the main purpose of some of these climate-sceptic bodies was to sow confusion in the minds of the public about climate science, so that any government action could be delayed or stopped. Manufacturing doubt or uncertainty, whether it is about the smoking–cancer link or climate science, so the argument goes, is one of the best ways of establishing a controversy.[75]

George Monbiot's book, *Heat*, examines how one of the first corporate campaigns in the early 1990s in the USA to deny anthropogenic global warming was initiated by a US tobacco company, Philip Morris.[76] He documents how the company hired a public relations company, APCO, who recommended to Philip Morris that a citizens' group should be funded to comment not just on tobacco-related issues, but on a series of broader government regulations resulting from such issues as global warming, nuclear waste disposal, and biotechnology.

Several studies since then have documented the role of other US companies, and in particular the oil giant ExxonMobil, and its financial links with think tanks and other lobby groups which espouse different types of climate change scepticism. The Royal Society in the UK, the Union of Concerned Scientists (UCS) in the US, and Greenpeace have all charted Exxon's involvement with different conservative or libertarian think tanks, including the Washington-based Cato Institute, the Competitive Enterprise Institute, the American Enterprise Institute, and the Heritage Foundation.[77] In 2008 Exxon said they no longer were funding some of the climate change sceptics, although some reports suggest its funding did continue after that year.[78] Other reports have cast the net wider to examine the somewhat murky links between other fossil fuel companies, individual scientists, and lobby groups, again mostly located in the US. Greenpeace for example has tracked the concerted efforts to campaign against the IPCC reports which started in 1990.[79]

One of the central arguments in Oreskes and Conway's book is that 'the link that unites the tobacco industry, conservative think tanks, and the scientists in our story is the defense of the free market'. In other words, they authors say the four scientists they focus on (Seitz, Singer,

---

[75] Washington and Cook, *Climate Change Denial*, 72; Hoggan, *Climate Cover-Up*, ch. 2.

[76] Geroge Monbiot, *Heat: How to Stop the Planet Burning* (2006), summarised in Washington and Cook, *Climate Change Denial*, 76.

[77] Hoggan, *Climate Cover-Up*, 74–7 and passim; 'Royal Society tells Exxon: Stop Funding Climate Change Denial', *Guardian*, 20 Sept. 2006, and for the UCS see www.ucsusa.org/news/press_release/ ExxonMobil-GlobalWarming-tobacco.html.

[78] Andy Revkin, 'Skeptics Dispute Climate Worries and Each Other', *New York Times*, 8 Mar. 2009; Kate Sheppard, 'Did ExxonMobil Break its Promise to Stop Funding Climate Change Deniers?', *Mother Jones*, 28 June 2011; 'Think-Tanks Take Oil Money and Use it to Fund Climate Deniers', *Independent*, 7 Feb. 2010; and 'Scientists Offered Cash to Dispute Climate Study', *Guardian*, 2 Feb. 2007. Considerable time and energy continues to be spent on probing Exxon's role in funding individual and organised sceptics. See e.g. www.carbonbrief.org/blog/2011/04/900-papers-supporting-climate-scepticism-exxon-links.

[79] Greenpeace, *Dealing in Doubt*.

and two others) and the George C. Marshall Institute were driven in part by ideology, and specifically the desire not to have governments intervening and regulating the market place. Free-market ideology may well have had a major influence over the four scientists whose lives and thinking were shaped by the Cold War. But as we have seen from the example of Steve McIntyre, ideology is clearly not the main or even significant driver behind all climate sceptics.

McIntyre runs a popular sceptical website, Climate Audit. Another Canadian, Professor of Economics Ross McKitrick, who was the second most quoted sceptic scientist in our UK survey, is a regular contributor to the website. There are several other popular climate-sceptic websites based in North America. Anthony Watts, a radio weatherman in the USA, runs the website WattsUpWiththat.com. A 2008 study calculated that the site even then already had a readership of over 31,000 users.[80] The same study reported that, according to one blog aggregation site, four of the top 20 science bloggers were climate sceptics. The majority of the most popular sceptic (and mainstream science) sites are written from the United States or Canada. In the UK sceptic sites are fewer, but in the course of this research, we were told that a significant amount of the traffic that flows to one of the most prominent examples, James Delingpole's on the *Telegraph* website, comes from the USA.

It is almost a cliché that it is on the Web where climate scepticism is to be found in its most voluminous, raw, energetic, witty – but also often personally abusive – form.[81] The Pew Center Project for Excellence in Journalism (PEJ) has shown how in the USA topics involving global warming have gained a much greater share of what the PEJ calls the 'news hole' in new media, including blogs, than in the traditional media like television, radio, and newspapers.[82] For example, it found that global warming/climate change was one of the top five blog stories during 13 different weeks since monitoring began in January 2009, at a time when it featured much less prominently in the traditional media. Likewise, studies of Twitter in the USA show that global warming is one of the most popular topics to be followed.[83] It is also in the USA where internet organising and web-based campaigning by both pro-environment and climate sceptic groups is probably most developed. For example, the Americans for Prosperity campaigning group, which receives funding from the Koch Family Foundation, is presented by media academics as an example of a climate-sceptic group gaining an amplified contrarian presence through the Web.[84]

---

[80] The study compared it with the circulation of the UK weekly, *New Statesman* (around 26,000 at the time), but it also did well compared to the 2009 circulation of the US weekly, *New Republic*, of 53,000. See Alex Lockwood, 'Seeding Doubt: How Sceptics Use New Media to Delay Action on Climate Change', paper presented to the Association for Journalism Education annual conference, Sheffield University (12 Sept. 2008).

[81] The British media academic Neil Gavin is doubtful of its merits and has described it as the 'rantosphere'. See e.g. his chapter 'The Web and Climate Change Politics: Lessons from Britain', in Boyce and Lewis (eds), *Climate Change and the Media*.

[82] Quoted in Boykoff, 'Public Enemy No. 1?'

[83] Presentation by Max Boykoff, Oxford, 14 July 2011.

[84] Boykoff, 'Public Enemy No. 1?', quoting J. Mayer, 'Covert Operations: The Billionaire Brothers who are Waging a War Against Obama', *New Yorker*, 30 Aug. 2010.

The final element as to why climate scepticism has flourished in the USA is related to the funding of American politicians by industry groups and the pervasive practice and power of lobbying. Both are common in other countries but the extent of them is probably unique to American political culture.[85] The multi-million dollar donations paid by oil, gas, and mining companies to individual members of Congress have been well documented, and often criticised.[86] The power of the lobbyists has also been well researched. According to figures from the US Center for Responsive Politics, in 2009 there were more than 13,000 officially registered lobbyists on a variety of issues who received US$3.5bn in fees.[87] In the particular case of energy policy, more oxygen is given to the lobbying efforts as particular states with strong links to the oil and gas industry, such as Texas, Wyoming, and Virginia, rally popular and Congressional support.[88] What is particularly striking is the growth in the number of lobbyists working on climate change who stand on different sides of the policy debates. According to the Center for Public Integrity, their number had increased to 2,340 in 2009 – an increase of 300% over the previous five years. This meant Washington had more than four climate lobbyists for every member of Congress.[89] Together, they were paid US$90m in 2008, although according to the Center this is a vast underestimate. Part of the 14% increase just in the first quarter of 2009 compared to 2008 was driven by the debate about cap-and-trade legislation.

Another recent study concluded that in 2009 the major conservative think tanks, advocacy groups, and industry associations in the USA spent an estimated US$259m on activities related to climate change and energy policy.[90] This compared with the US$394m pro-environment groups spent in the same year, according to the same report. The apparent outspending by the pro-environment groups has been hotly contested by critics of the report.[91] What is not in dispute is the huge sum of money available to groups located at the nexus of politics, policy, and climate change, which includes the various types of climate sceptics.

In summary, a strong case can be made that climate scepticism is a manifestation of American exceptionalism, although not in the sense

---

[85] Lobby groups are of course active in many other political systems. In July 2011, the Climate Change minister in the UK, Christopher Huhne, ordered a private inquiry into the influence of fossil fuel lobbyists over Conservative MEPs who had voted against ambitious emissions targets in the EU. *Guardian*, 23 July 2011.

[86] See e.g. Hoggan, *Climate Cover-Up*, ch. 13.

[87] Dmitry Denisov, 'Business Lobbying and Government Relations in Russia: The Need for New Principles', RISJ paper 2011, p. 21: http://reutersinstitute.politics.ox.ac.uk/fileadmin/documents/Publications/fellows__papers/2010-2011/Business_lobbying_and_government_relations_in_Russia.pdf.

[88] See Sheila McNulty, 'US Energy Industry Stages Rally Against Climate Bill', *Financial Times*, 18 Aug. 2009.

[89] www.publicintegrity.org/investigations/climate_change/articles/entry/1171/.

[90] Matthew Nisbet, *Climate Shift: Clear Vision for the Next Decade of Public Debate*, American University School of Communication, 2011, p. 5, available at http://climateshiftproject.org/report/climate-shift-clear-vision-for-the-next-decade-of-public-debate/.

[91] See e.g. Joe Romm, '*Climate Shift* Data Reanalysis Makes Clear Opponents of Climate Bill Far Outspent Environmentalists', 19 Apr. 2011: http://thinkprogress.org/romm/2011/04/19/207910/climate-shift-data-reanalysis.

that many authors have written and argued about.[92] We mean it purely in the context of the climate change: in the USA scepticism has a longer history, is better funded and organised, and is more deeply interwoven into the fabric of politics, ideology, and culture than it is in Europe and the rest of the world. It is also where the media-related activities of sceptical individuals and groups have historically been successful in getting coverage in the mainstream press.

Climate scepticism outside the USA

Although the USA is regarded as 'exceptional' in many ways, it does share with Australia and Britain the presence of large, privately owned oil, coal, and mining companies which have much to lose – arguably the most – by international or national legislation enforcing cuts in carbon emissions or a major switch to renewable sources of energy. It is of course a high stakes game particularly in the USA and Australia, where these companies would be doing more of the sacrificing than other sectors as a result of proposed cap-and-trade legislation or carbon taxes. In contrast, the number of privately owned oil and coal companies who would lose out is much fewer in countries like Brazil, India, and France where organised climate scepticism is hardly present. It would be hard to deny any correlation between the presence of oil and mining companies and the presence of organised (and public) climate scepticism.

In the case of Australia, coal is particularly important as the country is the world's largest exporter. About 80% of the country's electricity is generated from it. The relationship between the coal industry there and the media around the issue of climate change has been studied by two Australian academics, who write that 'it is impossible to understand the way that coal industry members act to secure their political and economic interests without considering their relationship to journalists and their activities in the media field'.[93] They and others have monitored the links between private climate-sceptic groups like the Lavoisier group and mining interests. However, it is also worth resisting too crude a characterisation of all oil, coal, and mining companies as promoting climate scepticism. Journalists and academic research have long documented major differences both between energy companies in attitudes towards global warming within the same country and between oil companies in Europe and the United States.[94] For example, in the

---

[92] Alexis de Tocqueville was apparently the first to describe the USA in such terms, because it had developed a uniquely American ideology, based on liberty, egalitarianism, individualism, populism, and laissez-faire. The former head of the RISJ journalism programme, Godfrey Hodgson, has written a critique of US exceptionalism: *The Myth of American Exceptionalism* (New Haven, CT: Yale University Press, 2009).

[93] Wendy Bacon and Chris Nash, 'Playing the Media Game: The Relative (In)Visibility of Coal Industry Interests in Media Reporting of Coal as a Climate Change Issue in Australia', paper presented at the ECREA conference, Hamburg 11–12 Oct. 2010.

[94] See e.g. David L. Levy and Ans Kolk (2002) 'Strategic Responses to Global Climate Change: Conflicting Pressures on Multinationals in the Oil Industry', *Business and Politics*, 4/3 (2002), 275–300; and for the differences between US energy companies, see Anna Fifield, 'US companies at odds over green lobbying', *Financial Times*, 29 Sept. 2009.

USA, Exxon's anti-global warming approach has at times been sharply different from that of other US oil companies, while in Australia the largest mining group BHP has announced it was in favour of a carbon tax, a policy at variance with the approach of other mining companies there.[95]

There is some evidence for thinking that organised scepticism, often with funding from vested interests, has expanded from the USA into other countries. Recent studies about 'the denial industry' suggest that think tanks strongly linked to individual sceptical scientists are now firmly established in the UK, Canada, and Australia.[96] In Canada, the free-market think tank Fraser Institute with key support from Professor McKitrick and other sceptics has been particularly vocal, while in Australia the Institute for Public Affairs has played a similar role.[97] In the UK the Global Warming Policy Foundation (GWPF), which says it is not a free-market think tank but a non-partisan educational charity, was set up in November 2009. These organisations are mostly found in English-speaking countries, which is one of the reasons why sceptics are quoted more in the media of these countries.

More research is needed into the links between US think tanks, fossil fuel companies, climate scientists, and the funding of similar think tanks in other countries. Several lists of prominent sceptics have been published in newspapers and campaign documents, but these lists sometimes suffer from a 'name and shame' approach and tone.[98] However, they do illustrate the high international profile of a relatively limited number of sceptic scientists and their links to think tanks outside their home country in the USA, the UK, or Canada. Many have been on speaking tours outside their own countries. For example, Patrick Michaels did a tour of Australia in August 2009.[99] The Galileo movement, which is a libertarian group set up in 2011 to promote the denial of the human causes of global warming, organised Lord Monckton's trip to Australia in 2011.[100]

The Australian sceptic and geologist, Professor Ian Plimer from the University of Adelaide, author of the popular sceptical book *Heaven and Earth*, was widely quoted in the UK press when he came on a speaking tour in December 2009 to promote his book.[101] This was one of the reasons why Professor Plimer was the most quoted sceptic scientist in our survey of the UK press, twice as many times as the most quoted British sceptic scientist, Philip Stott, who is a professor of biogeography.

---

[95] www.greentimes.com.au/climate-change/bhp-ndash-the-climate-change-catalyst-for-australia.html.
[96] Dunlap and McCright, 'Climate Change Denial', 250.
[97] According to the *Independent on Sunday*, the free-market Atlas (Economic Research) Foundation, which is based in the USA, has supported more than 30 think tanks around the world that espouse climate change scepticism: www.independent.co.uk/environment/climate-change/thinktanks-take-oil-money-and-use-it-to-fund-climate-deniers-1891747.html.
[98] See Larson and Keating, 'The FP Guide to Climate Skeptics'; 'The Coalition of Denial', *Guardian*, 4 Dec. 2009; 'A Field Guide to Climate Change Skeptics', *Mother Jones*, 21 Apr. 2011; a list of sceptical organisations can be found in the Appendix of Washington and Cook, *Climate Change Denial*.
[99] Greenpeace, *Dealing in Doubt*, n. 132.
[100] See 'How Climate Science Deniers Spread Doubt for Political Ends', *Climate Progress*, 4 July 2011.
[101] A detailed rebuttal of the arguments in Plimer's book can be found in Washington and Cook, *Climate Change Denial*, 80–6.

Mainstream scientists of course make many international speaking tours too. But it is doubtful whether a Danish or Australian mainstream climate scientist would be as well-known or as quoted as much in the UK press as a Danish or Australian sceptic like Bjørn Lomborg or Professor Plimer. Likewise, it would be surprising if a British climate scientist with an established peer-reviewed record of publications on climate science would get as much media attention in the USA and Australia as the UK sceptic Lord Monckton, who is not known to have published in peer-reviewed science journals.

The UK, Australia, France, India, and other countries do have right-wing think tanks linked to climate change scepticism, but probably not to the extent seen in the USA. That is in part because these countries do not have a tradition of political think tanks ingrained into the body politic to the same degree as in the USA. In France for example, there are such think tanks but they tend to be clubs created to support individual politicians.[102] And in the UK, the Institute for Economic Affairs and the Centre for Policy Studies have been associated with climate-sceptical positions (whereas the left-wing Institute for Public Policy Research, for example, studies, and urges action on, climate change as part of its programme), but they had little impact on the UK media. However, the situation changed with the launch of the London-based Global Warming Policy Foundation (GWPF).

Its two main spokesmen are the former Conservative Chancellor of the Exchequer under Margaret Thatcher, Lord Nigel Lawson, and its executive director, Dr Benny Peiser. It has cross-party support on its board of trustees with two Labour Lords, a Liberal Democrat Baroness, and two crossbenchers, also in the House of Lords. Their official view is that the basic science of global warming is sound, but the pace and extent of the impacts are uncertain. As Lord Lawson wrote in the *Daily Mail* on 11 June 2011, 'while it is scientifically established that increased emissions of carbon dioxide into the atmosphere … can be expected to warm the planet, it is uncertain how great any such warming would be, and how much harm, if any, it would do'. Critics say they do not stay aloof from the science, as they regularly distribute information to journalists and other interested parties about new research or findings that are at variance with mainstream climate science. But Dr Peiser is keen to stress that their main concern is about policy, because in his words, 'we are not deniers about the role of CO_2. But even if the IPCC is right, it does not tell anyone what to do about it.'[103] It specifically aims to criticise those, like the previous Labour Government and the coalition government of David Cameron, who believe it is necessary to spend large sums of money to decarbonise the UK economy.

The GWPF list of academic advisers is heavily stacked towards the sceptic end of the debate on causes, impacts, and what policy options to

[102] One example is Jean-Francois Cope's Generation France. See www. generationfrance.net/web/index. php/le-club-generation-france.html.
[103] Author interview, July 2011.

33

favour. It is interesting for the purposes of this study to note that many of the world's best known sceptics appear as advisers, including Professors Bob Carter and Ian Plimer from Australia, Vincent Courtillot from France, Freeman Dyson, William Happer and Richard Lindzen from the USA, Ross McKitrick from Canada, as well as two British professors, Paul Reiter and Philip Stott.[104] According to Dr Peiser, 'it is true that they are stacked towards the sceptical end, but they do not necessarily represent our views which are much broader'. It is not clear whether the GWPF receives international funding as it does not reveal the identity of its donors. It has been criticised for this lack of full disclosure particularly as it has been critical of the lack of transparency and scrutiny of climate scientists. Its public position is that it has not received money from the energy industry or anyone with a significant interest in it, but it declines to publish the identity of donors or how much individuals give, for fear that those individuals would be subject to public vilification.[105]

As regards the media, the GWPF says it is concerned with restoring more 'balance' in the coverage of climate change. They have had considerable success in getting their point of view across in much of the media. They are frequently seen or heard on the BBC, and as our survey shows, have been extensively quoted in the print media of all political colours. Lord Lawson and Dr Peiser were the two most quoted sceptics in our period of research – by some margin. (See Chapter 6.) The two also travel abroad to speak at international meetings. Lord Lawson toured Australia in 2011 and Dr Peiser was a speaker at an event organised by the American Freedom Alliance in June of the same year.

In this chapter we have highlighted the historical roots to scepticism in the USA, the presence of conservative think tanks with ties to interested economic groups, the strength of climate scepticism on the blogosphere, and the huge sums of money tied up in political lobbying. We have also highlighted how in the USA climate scepticism forms a much more significant part of the ideology of one of the two main political parties. As we shall see in the country-specific sections in Chapter 5, many of these factors are not replicated in other countries, either at all or to a much less significant degree, which in part explains the relative absence of climate-sceptic voices in these countries' media.

---

[104] It is interesting to note that the Galileo movement in Australia also opts for a number of international sceptics on its 'independent climate science group', including Lord Monckton, and Fred Singer (in addition to Plimer and Carter).

[105] Leo Hickman, 'Global Warming Policy Foundation Donor Funding Levels Revealed', *Guardian*, 20 Jan. 2011. According to the article, its total income for the period up to 31 July 2010 was £503,302.

3. Climate Scepticism in the Media

The previous chapter laid out some of reasons why and how climate change scepticism is deeply entrenched, well-funded, and well-organised in the United States. The argument was that in some ways the USA is 'exceptional'. Some observers would want to add that, in the world of the media too, the USA is unusual for the presence of opinionated journalism found on broadcast channels which is epitomised by the successful cable station, Fox News. As its critics argue, in both its news reporting and opinion pieces, its presenters and personalities openly and constantly reject mainstream climate science and regularly use exceptional cold winters to cast doubt on whether global warming is taking place.[106] This is combined with the framing of the debate about climate change as one about politics, not science, or at times as a battle between two evenly matched groups of scientists.[107]

The Fairness Doctrine which required broadcasting companies to be 'honest, fair and balanced' in the presentation of controversial issues of public importance, was abolished by the Reagan administration in 1987 and paved the way not just for Fox News but for other channels with a clear political preference like the left-leaning MSNBC. There are also no external regulations in the USA about accuracy. In contrast, both commercial and state TV and radio stations in the UK and Australia have to meet either internally imposed or external regulation on fairness and balance. However, the difference between the USA and the rest of the world on the prevalence of opinionated news in traditional media may not be as great as critics of the US would maintain: most of the US print media have strongly observed professional codes of practice with firewalls between news reporting and opinion or editorial pieces, whereas in the UK, Australia, and across Europe and the developing world overt political partisanship is commonplace in both tabloid and

---

[106] See e.g. Jocelyn Fong and Fae Jencks, 'Report Glosses over Media Failures in Climate Coverage', *MediaMatters*, 18 Apr. 2011, p.2. Mainstream climate scientists say 30-year trends and not individual (cold) winters are the appropriate time span to look for signs of global warming. Fox News' defence is that it is 'fair and balanced', by which it often means it is an essential corrective to what it says is the liberal bias of the main network stations.

[107] David McKnight, 'A Change in the Climate? The Journalism of Opinion at News Corporation', *Journalism*, 11 (2010), 697.

broadsheet newspapers. Moreover, in some European countries like Italy state channels are aligned with different political parties, while in India very few of the 80-plus 24/7 news channels that have emerged in recent years take an objective view on news.[108]

So is there any evidence that climate change scepticism is any more prevalent in the US media, or indeed in the wider Anglo-Saxon media, compared to the rest of the world? Given the exceptional characteristics of climate scepticism in the USA, including the greater presence of think tanks with well-funded media strategies, one would assume the answer is yes. But there are few studies which have focused specifically on the prevalence of sceptical voices, either in the USA or in other countries, or the comparisons between them, which can give a clear answer to this question. As the British media academic Neil Gavin has pointed out, most studies of organised or 'mobilised' scepticism offer only anecdotal evidence about coverage, 'without studying the treatment of climate scepticism in detail'.[109]

What there are in abundance in the academic literature are studies of the more general nature of the content of media coverage, and in particular the question of 'false balance'. Much of it has focused historically more on the USA than other countries.[110] The methodology commonly applied aims to capture the difference between those articles or reports which (1) present the viewpoint that anthropogenic global warming (AGW) accounts for all climate changes, (2) present multiple viewpoints, but emphasise that anthropogenic contributions significantly contribute to climate changes, (3) give a 'balanced account' surrounding the existence and non-existence of AGW, and (4) present multiple viewpoints but emphasise the claim that the anthropogenic component contributes negligibly to changes in the climate.[111] Category (2) is regarded as best capturing mainstream science, while category (3) captures those articles which give roughly equal attention and emphasis to competing views. Category (4) is where sceptic, denialist, or contrarian views would be most represented. The three most common categories – i.e. (2) to (4) – are often summarised as the 'consensus view' (climate change is real and human-caused), the 'falsely balanced view' (we don't know if climate change is real, or if humans are a cause), and the 'dismissive view' (climate change is not happening, or there is no role for humans).[112] Such a methodology usually goes beyond just counting the frequency of words, phrases, and viewpoints to include salience, tone, and tenor and other criteria which together give a more nuanced set of results than merely assessing the prevalence of sceptical voices.

As mentioned in Chapter 1, Max Boykoff and his brother Jules blazed a trail by applying this broad methodology to four US quality

---

[108] 'The Foxification of News', *The Economist*, 7 July 2011: www.economist.com/node/18904112.
[109] Neil Gavin and Tom Marshall, 'Mediated Climate Change in Britain: Scepticism on the Web and on Television around Copenhagen', *Global Environmental Change*, 21 (2011), 1035–44. The article includes a list of the academic literature that exists.
[110] See Painter, *Summoned by Science*, 13–15.
[111] Maxwell T. Boykoff and Maria Mansfield, '"Ye Olde Hot Aire": Reporting on Human Contributions to Climate Change in the UK Tabloid Press', *Environmental Research Letters*, 3 (2008), 4.
[112] See e.g. Nisbet, *Climate Shift*, 70.

print media from 1998 to 2002 focusing on how much they reflected the mainstream scientific consensus on climate change. Their famous conclusion – quoted in Al Gore's film *An Inconvenient Truth* – that more than half of the articles they examined gave equal coverage to views that it was due to humans or was natural (category (3) above) led to their use of the oxymoronic phrase 'balance as bias'. This article is still being quoted by global warming believers who want to criticise US media coverage,[113] even though Max Boykoff went on to show that the coverage in the quality press in the USA changed in subsequent years. His later research (this time of five prestige newspapers) showed that whereas 'US media representations of anthropogenic climate change diverged significantly from the scientific consensus in 2003 and 2004, … this was no longer significant in 2005 and 2006.'[114] The percentage had dropped to just 8% in 2006.[115] Boykoff attributed this change to a number of important events, including the growing recognition by scientists and President George W. Bush of the role greenhouse gases were playing in heating up the Earth.[116]

His study of British prestige newspapers in the same period also showed 'no evidence that the UK newspapers carried out informationally-biased coverage of anthropogenic climate change through the employment of the journalistic norm of "balanced" reporting'.[117] This led to his conclusion that he and others may have been 'flogging a dead norm'. Some commentators have pointed out that his research was partial as it only included the *Guardian, The Times*, the *Independent*, and their Sunday stablemates, and not the *Mail* and *Telegraph* daily and Sunday editions where many of the sources of coverage that have denied the human contribution to climate change are found.[118] Another criticism was that the research focused on the news reporting of these newspapers which reflected the consensus view (as it was often prompted by new scientific reports) and not the opinion or editorial pieces, which were less consistent with this view.

Boykoff's further research (with Maria Mansfield) concentrated on the news articles in four main British tabloids and their Sunday sister papers (the *Sun*, the *Mail*, the *Express*, and the *Mirror*) over the period 2000–6.[119] They concluded that the UK tabloid coverage significantly diverged from the scientific consensus, which contrasted with previous findings from his studies of the prestige press in the UK and the USA. This divergence was said to be in general driven by two factors – journalistic norms of balance, and the presence of contrarian views (claiming that

---

[113] See e.g. Washington and Cook, *Climate Change Denial*, 94.
[114] In their 2004 study, the Boykoffs included the *New York Times*, the *Wall Street Journal*, the *Washington Post*, and the *LA Times*. See Boykoff and Boykoff, 'Balance as Bias'. In the later study, the *USA Today* was added. See Maxwell T. Boykoff, 'Flogging a Dead Norm? Newspaper Coverage of Anthropogenic Climate Change In the United States and United Kingdom from 2003 to 2006', *Area*, 39/4 (2007), 474.
[115] Boykoff and Mansfield, 'Ye Olde Hot Aire', 4.
[116] Maxwell Boykoff, 'U.S. Climate Coverage in the '000s', *FAIR*, Feb. 2010, 2.
[117] Boykoff, 'Flogging a Dead Norm', 475.
[118] Ward, 'Climate Change, the Public, and the Media in the UK', in Boyce and Lewis (eds), *Climate Change and the Media*, 61–2.
[119] Boykoff and Mansfield, 'Ye Olde Hot Aire'.

humans' role in climate change is negligible).[120] Of the four newspapers, the left-leaning *Mirror* group had the highest percentage of coverage depicting a significant human contribution to climate change (87%), followed by the *Express* (81%), the *Sun* (80%) and the *Mail* (67%). The authors suggested that the general ideological stance of the newspapers partly explained the differences, but also concluded that in general 'inaccurate reporting may be linked to the lack of specialist journalists in the tabloid press'. In 2011 Boykoff wrote that in general his research has shown that that 'minority views – such as contrarian, skeptical or denialist discourses – earned more attention than was warranted by appraising the distribution views of the wider scientific community'.[121]

The debate rages on about how well the media in the UK and the USA are covering the scientific consensus, and within that debate, how much space is or should be given to sceptical voices. For example, the 2011 report on the US print media mentioned in the previous chapter, called *Climate Shift*, stirred up a huge furore. In Chapter 3 of the report, the author Matthew Nisbet concluded from his analysis of five mainstream sources of news (which included the *New York Times*, the *Washington Post*, and *Wall Street Journal*) in 2009 and 2010 that these media had moved past the much-criticised 'he-said, she-said' mode of false balance. The *Wall Street Journal*, and particularly its opinion pages, was an exception, but in general the reporting reflected the consensus science.

Criticism of Nisbet's report focused on the reporting of the *Washington Post* over the period, which included in 2009 opinion pieces by climate sceptics Bjørn Lomborg, the US Republican politician Sarah Palin, and George Will, who particularly attracted the wrath of the believers in man-made global warming.[122] One constant critic of the US mainstream coverage of climate change (in part for including too many sceptic voices), Joe Romm of the Climate Progress website, redid the content analysis using a different search engine over the same period to conclude that the *Post*'s news articles that reflected the consensus view amounted to a significantly lower figure (76% compared to 93%), thus casting doubt on the finding that 'false balance' was no longer present at the *Post*.[123]

Another of the criticisms of the *Climate Shift* report was that it did not include any TV coverage of climate change over the period. The liberal group Media Matters lambasted it for not including Fox News, which it pointed out was trusted by Republican voters more than any other major TV news outlet.[124] Research, again by Max Boykoff, has

---

[120] See 'Media Coverage of Climate Change "Divergent from Scientific Consensus",' *environmental researchweb*, 28 Apr. 2008.

[121] Boykoff, 'Public Enemy No. 1?', 7

[122] George Will wrote an opinion piece in the *Washington Post*, 15 Feb. 2009, which argued that predictions of dire, planetary impacts – drought, sea-level rise, etc. – caused by global warming were grossly exaggerated. The article caused much debate in media and climate change circles and led the CJR to call it 'The George Will Affair': www.cjr.org/the_observatory/the_george_will_affair.php .

[123] *Climate Progress*, 6 May 2011.

[124] Fong and Jencks, 'Report Glosses over Media Failures in Climate Coverage'. Matthew Nisbet's defence of why he did not include Fox News can be found in John Wihbey, 'Reviewing the Nisbet "Climate Shift" Report and Controversial Claims of Media Progress', *Yale Forum on Climate Change*

shown that, in the period 1995–2004, US television coverage of climate change represented a very large divergence from the consensus science, which was greater than that found in the prestige print media: only 28% depicted the human contribution to climate change as significant, whilst 72% diverged significantly from the mainstream consensus.[125] The years were described by Boykoff as the 'lost decade' of US television coverage of climate change.

The dispute about the *Climate Shift* report neatly illustrates just how contested even academic findings about climate change and the media have become in the USA. Much of the criticism of journalists and media comes from activists of both sceptic and anti-sceptic leanings and policy-makers who find the media an easy target when they feel public opinion or policy issues are not going their way. It is a point emphasised by the CJR's Curtis Brainard who argues that the news reporting of climate change in the mainstream media in the USA has travelled a long way from the days of 'false balance' before 2006. He says the way climate science is reported now is much more sophisticated than then as many reporters struggle with the specific consequences of climate change and the highly uncertain and nuanced science underlying them.[126] 'Overall I would say that coverage of climate scepticism is a relatively minor problem', says Brainard.

> *Almost all the US newspapers now report the science straight; they just don't cover it prominently or enough. There are some opinion pages like in the Journal that display scepticism but you don't see the same issues with climate sceptics quoted in news stories that you did six years ago. The exception is Fox News which is absolutely terrible and has a large reach.[127]*

There is also a vigorous debate in Australia about 'balanced coverage' and the appropriate amount of space to be given to climate sceptics in the media. This is largely because climate change policy, and particularly a carbon tax, has arguably been the most important political issue there since 2007 and has been amply debated in the media. The politics of climate change was a key factor in the defeat of the former Prime Minister John Howard in 2007, and the demise of another former prime minister, Kevin Rudd, and of two Opposition leaders. In 2009, climate change got more mentions in the media than any other issue, including

and the Media, 11 July 2011.
[125] M. Boykoff, 'Lost in Translation?, United States Television News Coverage of Anthropogenic Climate Change, 1995–2004', Climatic Change, 1–2 (2008), 1–17, quoted in Boyce and Lewis (eds), *Climate Change and the Media*, 97.
[126] As quoted in Wihbey, 'Reviewing the Nisbet "Climate Shift" Report'.
[127] Author interview, July 2011. In 2010 Fox News had an audience of around 4.1m viewers per night, lower than the three networks (ABC, CBS, and NBC) which each get about 5.5–8.5m for a total of 21.6m. But Fox is the largest cable TV network. See http://stateofthemedia.org/2011/network-essay/data-page-5.

the global financial crisis.[128] Two Australian media academics, Philip Chubb and Chris Nash, summarise the prevalence of sceptics in the media like this:

> *While an overwhelming majority of Australians believe in the scientific evidence for anthropogenic climate change, there has also been an outspoken cluster of denialists and sceptics, supported by a campaigning media, particularly those newspapers owned by Rupert Murdoch's News Ltd, which accounts for approximately 70% of Australia's national and metropolitan newspaper market. The News Ltd national broadsheet The Australian and major tabloids The Daily Telegraph (Sydney) and The Herald Sun (Melbourne) have campaigned tirelessly to throw doubt on climate change science and the bona fides of climate scientists, along the way launching some climate change denialists to celebrity status.[129]*

Among those the authors describe as a 'celebrity denialist' is Lord Monckton, whom we highlighted in Chapter 2. According to content analysis carried out by the authors of his tour to Australia in January and February 2010, Monckton received saturation coverage on the various outlets of the state broadcaster, ABC. Much of it they said was uncritical. They also pointed to the many fewer times Dr James Hansen, director of NASA's Goddard Institute for Space Studies and a 'radical' on climate science, appeared on ABC during his visit to Australia shortly afterwards; 5 compared to the 47 for Monckton over a comparable time period.[130] Commercial radio hosts also gave Monckton plenty of air space, which may partly explain why ABC felt compelled to do the same. A study by another Australian academic, David McKnight, who has written extensively about News Corporation, described one of the Murdoch-owned newspapers, *The Australian*, in the period 2001–7 as running editorials which tended to be sceptical, and carrying a large number of articles and columns which more sharply denied the science of climate change, 'often drawing on the arguments of the small group of fossil-fuel funded 'sceptical scientists'.[131]

The Canadian author and public relations consultant James Hoggan has also documented the strong presence of sceptical voices in parts of the media in his home country. In his book, *Climate Cover-Up*, he gives details of the considerable space given to a prominent climate sceptic, Professor Barry Cooper, who writes a regular column for the *Calgary Herald*. Calgary is capital of the province of Alberta, which is

---

[128] P. Chubb and C. Nash, 'The Politics of Reporting Climate Change at the Australian Broadcasting Corporation', paper presented at ECREA, Hamburg, Oct. 2010, p. 1.

[129] Ibid. 2.

[130] The authors do point out however that Monckton was challenged on about 50% of the primary occasions he appeared, whereas Hansen was never challenged by sceptics.

[131] McKnight, 'A change in the climate?', *Journalism*, 11 (2010), 693.

home to the largest of Canada's huge tar sand deposits. According to Hoggan, another prominent sceptic, Timothy Ball, a former professor of climatology at the University of Winnipeg who moved to work for a privately funded group called 'Friends of Science', is 'everywhere' in the Canadian media.[132]

The discussion above would seem to support the view that climate scepticism in the media is much more of an Anglo-Saxon phenomenon, at least in the USA, Australia, Canada, and the UK.[133] A provocative article on the Grist website has attempted to draw out some 'big picture' differences between the reporting of climate change in USA and continental Europe, suggesting that 'European media are from hothouse Venus, and their American counterparts from frigid Mars'.[134] Editors at major newspapers in Holland and Belgium quoted in the Grist article said that there was no debate in their countries about climate change, so sceptics were not quoted, whereas 'American news media still make the mistake of giving climate sceptics a disproportionate voice'.

There is evidence, for example, from academic research of the Belgian French press that little if any space is given to sceptical scientific voices. A study of 2,500 articles between 1997 and 2009 suggested that climate change was the scientific issue that received the largest press coverage. But 'contrary to the US media coverage of the climate change issue where journalists gave equal weight to the "believers" and the "skeptics", there was no opposition between "believers" and "skeptics" in the Belgian French press'.[135]

A study of the print media's treatment of climate change in Holland and France from 2001–7 reached a similar conclusion that the articles the researchers examined focused on 'scientific certainty and frequently referenced the responsibility for and the consequences of climate change'.[136] Likewise, a study of the German press also concluded that the emphasis was on scientific certainty and that climate sceptics hardly received any attention in the press there. This too prompted the authors of the Dutch and French study to posit the same thesis mentioned above that 'European media do not give the impression of scientific uncertainty concerning anthropogenic climate change as much as the US media do'.

The general picture may be true but there are clearly nuances and exceptions. As we will see in Chapter 6, there are parts of the UK media which give a lot more prominence to sceptics, and parts which don't. The same is true of the United States. What are interesting are the factors which explain these differences. And not all the European press is the same.

---

[132] Hoggan, *Climate Cover-Up*, 49, for Timothy Ball, and 157 for Barry Cooper.
[133] Greenpeace says that business groups in New Zealand have regularly hosted tours by well-known sceptics like Fred Singer and Lord Lawson. It also says that sceptics there have joined forces with Canadian and Australian sceptics to form the International Climate Science Coalition. Greenpeace, *Dealing in Doubt*, 15.
[134] Tom Vandyck, 'Unfair and Balanced: Is US Reporting Too Soft on Climate Sceptics?', *Grist*, 7 July 2011.
[135] Antigoni Vokou, 'Representing the Risks of Climate Change in the Belgian French Press: 1997–2009', paper presented at ECREA, Hamburg, Oct. 2010, p. 7.
[136] Boyce and Lewis (eds), *Climate Change and the Media*, ch. 16.

Recent studies of the Norwegian press for example suggest the sceptics get significant coverage there, in part because the second largest political party, the Progress Party, which is right-leaning, has a strong sceptical tendency within it.[137] The amount of coverage increased after the start of 'Climategate' (described in Appendix 1), which gave climate sceptics in Norway fresh ammunition to challenge the urgency and gravity of climate change.[138] This debate carried on throughout the spring of 2010.

What about the global south? The RISJ study of the media coverage of Copenhagen found that there were very few sceptic voices quoted at all during the summit, but when they were it was only in the Western press.[139] In all the 427 articles in 12 countries that were looked at, sceptics were quoted by name only twice – Professor Richard Lindzen in Italy's *Corriere della Sera*, and Steve McIntyre (whom we described in Chapter 2) in the *New York Times*. The RISJ study argued that its findings were consistent with a general trend of the media in G-77 developing countries quoting sceptics much less than the media in the Western press. It referred to several studies of individual country and regional findings:

- In China, the media seem to be less inclined than their Western counterparts to include the opposite opinion of everything that they are reporting on about climate change.

- A study of 147 articles published in the Indian press between January 2002 and June 2007 showed that no space was given to sceptics, and 98% of articles attributed climate change to anthropogenic causes.[140]

- In Peru, the media almost universally accepts anthropogenic climate change as reality.

- In the African media there is a near total absence of climate change contrarians. For example, in the case of Ghana, one study showed that print media had just one mention of a sceptic in the first six months of 2008.[141]

Anecdotal evidence from journalists attending the RISJ programme in recent years and other sources would suggest that the media in most

---

[137] CERES21 study forthcoming 2011, available via www.ceres21.org.
[138] e.g. on 31 Jan. 2010 the Progress Party leader Siv Jensen was emboldened to criticise the IPCC in an article in the leading newspaper *Aftenposten* under the headline 'No More Talk about Global Warming'.
[139] Painter, *Summoned by Science*, 51–2. A wider study of the Copenhagen summit by Eide et al. found that very few sceptical voices were quoted during the summit, and when present, they were mostly found in the opinion pages. Elisabeth Eide, Risto Kunelius, and Ville Kumpu (eds), *Global Climate, Local Journalisms* (Bochum/Freiburg: project verlag, 2010).
[140] S. Billet, 'Dividing Climate Change: Global Warming in the Indian Mass Media', *Climatic Change*. 99/1–2 (2009), 1–16.
[141] Paddy Coulter and Atle Midttun, *Escaping Climate Change: Climate Change in the Media. North and South Perspectives* (CERES, June 2009).

countries in Africa, Latin America, and Asia give little time to the sceptics, in part because, as many observe, their countries are at the forefront of experiencing the climate changing. An article in the *New Scientist* in March 2011 by a researcher at Cardiff University neatly summarised the situation in Uganda where more than 80% of the population are farmers, and are in little doubt the climate is changing.[142] The researcher Adam Corner wrote:

> *Opposing the scientific consensus on climate change has become something of an article of faith for the socially conservative religious right in the US. But in Uganda – a deeply religious and superstitious nation infamous for its rampant homophobia – climate change scepticism is nowhere to be seen. … The seasonal rains that once arrived with precision are now erratic and unpredictable. When your living depends on the fertility of your farmland, the climate is vitally important. In an office in London or New York it is less of a big deal.*

But the absence of climate scepticism in the global south is not simply a product of large rural populations experiencing a changing climate. In heavily urbanised South Korea for example, all three of the country's largest newspapers, which follow a conservative, progressive, and business orientation, 'accept climate change with little unjustified skepticism'.[143] Likewise, although there have been no studies of the presence of sceptical voices in the press in Brazil and Mexico, conversations with journalists there suggest again little questioning of the mainstream science. In both countries, this is linked to the virtual absence of scientists who are sceptical about climate change, but also to the high prominence of several scientists in public life and the media who follow the mainstream consensus. Mario Molina in Mexico, for example, who is a national hero and a winner of the Nobel Prize for chemistry, played a major role at the formal opening of the UN's Cancun talks on climate change in December 2010. The absence of sceptical lobby groups is in part due to the oil and energy sectors being mainly run by state-owned companies, PEMEX in Mexico and PETROBRAS in Brazil. This is a theme we will return to in the discussion of Brazil in Chapter 5.

The effect of 'Climategate'

Many of the studies quoted above came out before 'Climategate' and the questioning of the IPCC reports, the first of which really took off as a story in November 2009. (See Appendix 1.) For the media in some of

---

[142] Adam Corner, 'A Country with No Time for Climate Change Scepticism', *New Scientist*, 3 Mar. 2011.
[143] Robin Lloyd, 'Why are Americans So Ill-Informed on the Topic of Climate Change?', *Scientific American*, 23 Feb. 2011.

the Western press, and particularly in the US and UK, this was the time when sceptics received a lot more coverage, for very understandable journalistic reasons. The controversies had a profound impact – at least for a few months that followed – not just on scientists and environment activists but also on many journalists and editors. Roger Harrabin, one of the environment correspondents at the BBC, speaks of the 'different territory' the media reporting of climate change entered after 'Climategate'.[144] According to the journalist Fred Pearce, reporters at the BBC came under pressure to put more sceptics on the air. He quotes an anonymous correspondent as saying that the BBC was 'back to the false balance days that chiefs swore had been left behind'.[145]

There has been little content analysis done to prove any sustained change as a result of 'Climategate' to the BBC view that the 'weight of evidence no longer justifies equal space being given to the opponents of the consensus'.[146] A 2011 study of the quoting of sceptics in BBC and ITV late evening TV bulletins during the Copenhagen conference found that the BBC gave prominence to sceptic voices in two of their 22 bulletins (which were broadcast on the opening two days), including Lord Monckton speaking at a side conference.[147] The authors conclude that, 'although their messages did not figure prominently, it should be remembered that sceptics rarely seek to dominate debate, merely cloud it'. However, more research is needed to show a definitive shift from the pre-'Climategate' period.

But it is clear that for several UK correspondents regularly reporting on climate change 'Climategate' was a game changer, although this may well have fallen off after the official inquiries found the scientists had not manipulated or falsified data. A 2010 study by RISJ journalist fellow Margot O'Neill, from ABC in Australia, found that half of the ten British environment journalists she interviewed in mid-2010 were giving more space to sceptics, and four out of ten spoke of the effect on their editors who – in broad terms – wanted more questioning of the mainstream science. Interviews with British editors and journalists carried out for this study do clearly corroborate the view that for many of them, 'Climategate' did make them less trusting of mainstream science and more willing to test where there was sufficient consensus and where there was not. Some editors who were previously sceptical of some of the science and of their correspondents being too close to the environment movement were emboldened to push their correspondents and coverage in general to include more sceptical voices.

It is important to stress too that some interviewees spoke of the positive fall-out from 'Climategate' in the sense it was seen as a healthy

[144] Harrabin presentation at conference 'Carbonundrums: From Science to Headlines' held in Oslo, Feb. 2011.
[145] Pearce, *Climate Files*, 190. He says one of the beneficiaries of the BBC's new policy was Benny Peiser of the GWPF.
[146] As quoted in BBC Trust, *From Seesaw to Wagon Wheel: Safeguarding Impartiality in the 21st Century* (London: BBC, 2007), 40.
[147] Gavin and Marshall, 'Mediated Climate Change in Britain'.

corrective – inevitable in many of their eyes – to the overwhelming narrative of alarmism coming out from many NGOs and some climate scientists. As the *Independent* wrote in an editorial on 7 February 2010,

> *The climate change sceptics have done us all a favour. This may seem a curious view for a newspaper so committed to the cause of environmental sustainability. But, by challenging the consensus view of global warming, the sceptics have tested the flabbier assumptions of that consensus and forced the proponents of the majority view to sharpen their arguments.*

It is a view echoed not just amongst journalists at national newspapers, but in the minds of editors at the *New Scientist*. Deputy editor Graham Lawton says that 'Climategate' did not change their view that man-made global warming was happening and was a serious problem. But he adds that 'it was a reality check for us too. It made us less strident, less preachy and less policy prescriptive.'[148]

In the USA, 'Climategate' also received a considerable amount of coverage both in the prestige press and the broadcast media, at least compared to the media in many other countries. For example, the *New York Times* ran a front-page piece about it on 21 November 2009, while CNN ran two special segments on the two opening days of the Copenhagen conference. According to figures in the *Climate Shift* report, 54 of the articles in the five news outlets during December 2009 alone mentioned the stolen emails.[149] Prominent sceptics were quoted, causing some critics to complain that the mainstream media were returning to what they called the 'pernicious practice' of false balance.[150] Others have argued that a significant drop in the percentage of articles reflecting the scientific consensus after 'Climategate' in the *New York Times*, *Wall Street Journal,* and *Washington Post* (by 11%, 21%, and 5% respectively) was possibly due to the way 'Climategate' 'shifted the way the news outlets present the science, despite the fact that nothing in the leaked emails undermined the body of evidence supporting anthropogenic global warming'.[151] One journalist at the *Financial Times* described the *WSJ* (and the *Daily Telegraph*) in its column pieces of 'leading the charge' against mainstream science as a result of 'Climategate'. The author said one of the reasons was that such pieces were very popular with readers.[152]

There is strong evidence for thinking that 'Climategate' did receive much more coverage in parts of the Western press compared to the rest of the world, which would have increased the likelihood of more sceptical voices appearing. For example, a very extensive UN survey

[148] Author interview, June 2011.
[149] Fong and Jencks, 'Report Glosses over Media Failures in Climate Coverage', 3, quoting *Climate Shift* figures.
[150] Julie Hollar, '"Climategate" Overshadows Copenhagen'.
[151] Fong and Jencks, 'Report Glosses over Media Failures in Climate Coverage', 3.
[152] Kiran Stacey, 'Climategate and its Aftermath', *Financial Times*, 2 Dec. 2009.

of the media coverage of Copenhagen in 70 countries found that only 20% of the coverage on 'Climategate' during the summit originated in the global south.[153] However, there are probably important variations again between the Anglo-Saxon media and other countries in the Western world. For example, anecdotal evidence suggests it received much less attention in Germany and France, although in the former country the attacks on the IPCC may have had more play.[154] Likewise, in Portugal, 'Climategate' did not make much difference to the scant attention sceptics receive in the print media there. According to an experienced Portuguese environment journalist, this is due to the lack of organisation amongst sceptics, some of whom have been discredited, and the reluctance on the part of journalists to give them space.[155] We shall return to this discussion in Chapter 5.

In China two studies of the media there published in 2011 suggest that there was a small increase in the number of sceptical voices quoted after 'Climategate'. A CERES study covering the first six months of 2010 found that 2% of all the newspaper articles examined reflected scepticism about global warming – up from a zero finding in an earlier study conducted two years before.[156] This was in part a product of limited coverage of 'Climategate' and the questioning of the IPCC reports. In January 2010, shortly after 'Himalayagate' emerged, Xie Zhenhua, then China's top climate change envoy at UN talks, surprised many observers when he stated he was 'keeping an open mind on whether global warming was man-made or the result of natural cycles'. A report by chinadialogue found that 'scepticism of the climate-change consensus also appeared in some media outlets around that time, particularly in contributions from … Chinese climate-change-sceptic authors'.[157] In India, 'Himalayagate' rather than 'Climategate' made more impact as it was much more of an Indian story.

Before finishing this chapter, it is worth making a brief mention of the possible correlation between the prevalence of sceptical voices in the media in different countries and the variations between those countries in public attitudes about the seriousness or certainty with which the general public hold the science of climate change.[158] It is interesting that Brazil, for example, often comes out as a country where the population is very concerned about climate change. A 2010 Gallup poll of more than 100 countries showed Brazil in fourth place (behind Greece, Ecuador, and Venezuela) with 78% of those asked believing that global warming represented a serious threat to their family.[159] This was a 2% increase

---

[153] UN Department of Public Information, *United Nations Climate Change Conference: Copenhagen 2009*, internal report (New York: UN, Sept. 2010), 3.
[154] Author email exchange with Stefan Rahmstorf, and interview with Yves Scamia.
[155] According to Ricardo Garcia, a former RISJ journalist fellow, 'The Expresso weekly is probably the newspaper that has dedicated more resources to sceptics – with both sceptics and non-sceptics be[ing] given the same editorial space in certain stories, interviews and op-eds'. Email exchange, July 2011.
[156] CERES21 study forthcoming 2011.
[157] Sam Geall, 'Climate-Change Journalism in China: Opportunities for International Cooperation', *chinadialogue* (2011), 33.
[158] For a wider discussion, see Painter, *Summoned by Science*, 73–5.
[159] www.gallup.com/poll/147203/Fewer-Americans-Europeans-View-Global-Warming-Threat.aspx#2.

from 2007–8, which compared to a *drop* of 10 points in the USA (from 63% to 53%), of 12 points in the UK (from 69% to 57%), and of 6 points (75% to 69%) in Australia over the same period. In general, concern in Latin American countries as a whole went up by 6% over the period (from 67% to 73%), as it did in sub-Saharan Africa by 5% (from a low base of 29% to 34%). In contrast, it dropped by 10% in the USA and Western Europe.

It would be tempting to jump to the conclusion that the media coverage or lack of it of 'Climategate' and the linked issue of the prevalence of sceptical voices was a major driver of the drop in the three Anglo-Saxon countries and a rise in the global south. But there are several problems with such an analysis. First, the relationship is complex between media coverage and its impact on people's beliefs on climate change, not least because of the multiple influences coming to bear on what affect anyone's standpoint beyond those of what he or she might read, see, or hear from the media. It might have been particularly cold winters for example in the USA and the UK which most affected peoples' attitudes.[160] Secondly, there is plenty of scholarly work examining the 'agenda-setting' role the media can play in getting people to think about an issue, but not necessarily what views they come to.[161] Next, as the Gallup researchers themselves pointed out,

> *world residents' declining concern about climate change may reflect increasing scepticism about global warming after 'Climategate' and the lack of progress toward global climate policy. The drops also may reflect the poor economic times, during which Gallup research generally finds environmental issues become less important.*

Finally, in France where, as we shall see, there was much less coverage of 'Climategate' and in general nothing like the amount of space given to climate-sceptic voices (at least in the print media) as in the UK, concern dropped by a greater percentage than in the UK (16% compared to 12%). Likewise, despite the drop in concern in Australia and the USA, the two countries still had a higher percentage of concern amongst the population than in Belgium, Sweden, and Finland – three European countries not known for the prevalence of sceptical voices in the media or public life.

---

[160] There is some evidence to think that 'Climategate' did not register much in the minds of the general UK population. Both in a 2010 BBC UK poll and in the 2010 poll carried out by researchers at Cardiff University, it seems few people had actually heard of 'Climategate', suggesting the impact of the media coverage had not been as significant (or bad in their view) as many scientists and policy-makers had suggested. See n. 23 for Cardiff University study, and http://news.bbc.co.uk/1/hi/8500443.stm for the BBC poll. Some argue that, while it may not have had much impact on what British people felt about the science, there is evidence to suggest that it had a significant impact on whether they trusted climate scientists to tell the truth about climate science: www.newscientist.com/blogs/thesword/2011/02/has-the-impact-of-climategate.html.

[161] See e.g. B.C. Cohen, *The Press and Foreign Policy* (Princeton, NJ: Princeton University Press, 1963).

So what can we say in conclusion?

- There have been few studies specifically on the prevalence of sceptical voices in the media of individual countries, or comparative studies between different countries. However, studies of the more general issue of 'false balance' would strongly suggest that the questioning of mainstream science is more of an Anglo-Saxon phenomenon, and is particularly prevalent in parts of the media in the USA, Australia, Canada, and the UK.

- However, within the media in the Anglo-Saxon countries there are nuances and important differences. There is some evidence for thinking that, for example, within the UK print media, there are important differences between tabloids and broadsheet newspapers in the reporting of climate change. Few studies have distinguished between straight news reporting and the opinion pages.

- Within the global south, there does seem to be a general trend of the media not offering as much space to sceptic voices as in parts of the Anglo-Saxon press.

- 'Climategate' was an important driver and shaper of the amount and type of coverage of climate change in some countries (like the UK and USA) but not in others. There is evidence for the significant effect it had on journalists and editors in the UK, at least in the immediate months following it, but few studies have mapped the nature and extent of any lasting change in outputs in the UK or anywhere else.

4. A Comparison of Climate Scepticism in the Print Media of Six Countries

In this chapter we now turn to the content analysis of the print media in six countries (Brazil, China, France, India, the United Kingdom, and the United States). General comparative results are given, followed by discussion of the individual countries in Chapters 5 and 6. As we saw in the preceding chapters, the role that Fox News in the USA and the BBC in the UK play in giving airtime (or not) to sceptical voices is hugely important. In general, a majority of people in many countries of the world still say their most popular source of news is television, and there is considerable evidence that it is the most trusted medium.[162] Even in the USA, research by the Pew Centre suggests that despite the rise of online information as a consumer choice for Americans' source of news, a majority still turn to television as their main source of news. Moreover, very few studies have included the coverage of climate change on television, in any country. So it is to be regretted that, for reasons of expediency, we too focused on print and not broadcast media.

In most cases, we concentrated on the print version of the newspaper and not those found on the newspaper's online site. This was also restrictive. As mentioned in Chapter 2, the presence of sceptical voices particularly on the comment pages is hugely significant and can attract considerable traffic to a website. Many of the commentaries don't make it into the print version of a newspaper. (See Appendix 3 for further discussion.) We have also mentioned already how, at least in the USA, global warming can figure more prominently on blogs than in the traditional media like newspapers. The symbiotic relationship between new and old media prompts all sorts of questions beyond the scope of this study, including whether new/social media provide more space for sceptic views to circulate and gain more traction than they might do if restricted to traditional newspapers.[163] However, as has been

---

[162] See Painter, *Summoned by Science*, 13–14 and Appendix 1.
[163] See Boykoff, 'Public Enemy No. 1?', 12.

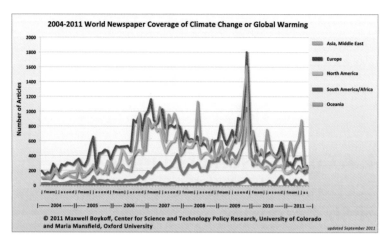

Figure 4.1. 2004–11 World Newspaper Coverage of Climate Change or Global Warming

argued elsewhere, print media have a strong agenda-setting influence on policy-makers and other elites, and in many media landscapes act as 'gatekeepers of information' and prompts for coverage in the other media, including TV and radio. In India, for example, TV journalists say their news agenda is often driven by newspaper stories.[164]

A team of researchers analysed print coverage from two three-month blocks, the first from 1 February to 30 April 2007 and the second from 19 November 2009 to 18 February 2010. These periods were chosen for several reasons: first, as can be seen from Figure 4.1, they broadly coincided with the two largest peaks in the amount of coverage of climate change or global warming in most of the world's print media for the period 2004 to July 2011. This was true of many countries but in particular for three of the six countries we chose – India, the UK, and the USA. Separate figures for these three countries available at the CIRES website on the University of Colorado, Boulder, website, show that the Indian coverage in four English-language newspapers (including the two we used) actually peaked at a slightly higher level in the early 2007 compared to late 2009/early 2010. In the case of eight UK newspapers (all of which are included in our survey), the highest peak was in the second period, followed by the second highest peak in the first period. In the USA, there were two large peaks in the middle of 2007 and at the end of 2009/early 2010, but there was still significantly high coverage in our first period.[165]

The second reason why we chose these two periods is that they included key moments in the recent narrative of the climate change story: in the first period, the release of the first two very influential IPCC reports of 2007 (known as WG-1 and WG-2 on 2 February

---

[164] See Painter, *Summoned by Science*, 14, and Max Boykoff, 'Indian Media Representations of Climate Change in a Threatened Journalistic Ecosystem', *Climatic Change*, 99 (2010), 17–25, 18.
[165] The individual country figures can be seen in Chs. 5 and 6 below. They are available via http://sciencepolicy.colorado.edu/media_coverage/us/index.html.

and 6 April respectively), in the UK the showing of a controversial and much discussed TV documentary on Channel 4 called the *Great Global Warming Swindle*, and in the USA, the dispute over the Environmental Protection Agency and efforts to control GHG emissions. The second period included 'Climategate', the Copenhagen summit, the controversies surrounding errors in the IPCC reports, a cold winter in many parts of the northern hemisphere, and in the case of the UK, the formation of the sceptical lobby group, the GWPF.

We deliberately chose two periods in which there was likely to have been a lot of coverage of climate change both in the news and the opinion pages. In the second period in particular, you would expect a significant amount of climate-sceptical voices as in many cases they led the criticism of the behaviour of scientists at the University of East Anglia and of the IPCC reports. As Andy Revkin the former environment correspondent at the *New York Times* says, 'There were several layers of obligations which any reporter on this piece would have had; not to seek input from people whose names came up in the emails would be irresponsible. It was an obligation for journalists to go to sceptics to cover that aspect of the story.'[166] Some of the media sought out different types of sceptics, who in turn took advantage of the moment and were emboldened to come out and speak to the media. An increase in the prevalence of sceptical voices gave us more material with which to map more effectively the differences between and within countries.

However, a note of caution should be raised as to just how much of the overall coverage 'Climategate' represented during the second period. As Max Boykoff has found, it was a 'hot button issue' during this time in the UK and US press, but still remained a 'relatively minor "signal" quantitatively over this period amidst the "noise" of overall climate change or global warming coverage.'[167] Certainly, it did not have much effect in stopping an overall trend of a sharp drop in coverage of climate change after our second period of study. In India's Anglophone press there was apparently another peak in early 2011, but several observers of the US and UK media have noted the sharp decline there in coverage in 2010–11, which some ascribed to 'climate fatigue' on the part of editors, journalists, and the public alike. For example, analysis by dailyclimate.org concluded that '2010 was the year climate coverage fell off the map'. Its database showed that the volume of coverage in English-language publications dropped by 30% from 2009, and back to 2005 levels. Research by Professor Robert Brulle at Drexel University showed that, for 2010, TV coverage in the US of climate change was minimal.[168] Certainly, environment journalists in the UK talk of searching for new angles and storylines from 2010 onwards to interest readers and viewers in the absence of the strong narrative provided by the Copenhagen summit and 'Climategate'.

[166] Author interview, July 2011.
[167] Boykoff, 'Public Enemy No. 1?', 3.
[168] See James Painter, 'Media Interest in Climate Change Takes a Dive', 11 Jan. 2011: http://politicsinspires.org/2011/01/media-interest-in-climate-change-takes-a-dive.

Part of the reason for the decline is also tied to the fact that many news organisations, at least in the USA, were suffering budget cuts affecting environment reporters. Shrinking budgets and more pressure on journalists to supply content across more media platforms may have had the effect of producing 'quick, cheap reporting, as well as discussion and commentary formats that rarely provide informative discussions of actual science results', as one US media expert described it in *Scientific American*.[169] These are important shapers of the general coverage of climate change, but in our sample of newspapers, it is our impression that they did not play a huge role. The *New York Times* and the *Wall Street Journal* remain well-resourced compared to the 1,400 newspapers in the USA who are cutting staff.

Methodology

The key research questions we were addressing in designing the content analysis were the following:

(1) Has been there an increase in the amount of space given to sceptics in the print media of different countries between the two research periods in 2007 and 2009/10?

(2) Are there important country variations?

(3) Are there any important differences between left-leaning and right-leaning newspapers in the prevalence of sceptical voices?

(4) In which part of a newspaper are sceptical voices most likely to be found?

(5) In broad terms, which types of sceptical voices are most included?

(6) What is the professional background of the sceptics who are quoted?

The answers to these questions prompted a series of other questions, and in particular what accounts for the differences between countries, and for the differences within the print media in the UK. These are addressed in Chapters 5 and 6.

The reasons for the selection of the six countries were because we wanted to include (a) countries where there is a strong presence of

---

[169] Robin Lloyd, 'Why are Americans So Ill-Informed on the Topic of Climate Change?', *Scientific American*, 23 Feb. 2011.

sceptical voices or lobby groups (the USA and the UK), (b) three of the emerging powers known as the BASIC countries (Brazil, India, and China), and (c) France, in part to include another developed country and in part to test if climate scepticism in the media is essentially an 'Anglo-Saxon phenomenon'.[170]

In each country we chose two newspapers with a right-leaning and left-leaning or liberal political slant, although this was not possible in China (where there are important differences in the print media in terms of business models, readership targets, and content, but few political differences). In the case of India, we would have preferred to have a paper in Hindi, but this proved impracticable.[171] Also, the division between the two newspapers there is not so much characterised by a left–right split. *The Hindu* is left-leaning but the *Times of India* is more centrist or liberal. So the choices of the two papers in each country were:[172]

Brazil: *Folha de São Paulo, Estado de São Paulo*

China: *People's Daily, Beijing Evening News*

France: *Le Monde, Le Figaro*

India: *The Hindu, Times of India*

United Kingdom: *Guardian/Observer, Telegraph/Sunday Telegraph*

United States: *New York Times, Wall Street Journal*

In the case of the United Kingdom, we expanded the number of newspapers to all ten major national newspapers, as described in Chapter 6.

Where possible, the researchers used the Lexis-Nexis or Factiva search facilities. The exceptions were China, where the researcher used the *People's Daily*'s own search engine and hard copies of the *Beijing Evening News* (as the newspaper doesn't have its own database), and in India where the search engines of the online editions were used (in the case of the *Times of India*, epaper.timesofindia.com, and in the case of *The Hindu*, www.thehindu.com). We also had to use the *Financial Times*' own search facility as the paper is not available via outside search engines. The key words 'climate change' or 'global warming' were entered with the additional filter of 'at the start' where this was possible.[173] In most

---

[170] Australia would have been an obvious choice to include but time and money did not allow it.
[171] The two largest Hindi-language newspapers, *Dainik Bhaskar* and *Dainik Jagran*, did not offer online archival facilities that extended as far back as 2007.
[172] Short profiles of these newspapers can be found in the following chapter.
[173] In the case of the *Financial Times*, we only included those articles where one of the two phrases appeared in the first four paragraphs, in an attempt to bring it more into line with the 'at the start' option.

cases, we were only looking at the articles that appeared in the print versions of the newspapers, and did not include the online versions.

We included news reports, features, opinion or comment pieces, editorials, and reviews (such as TV or book reviews). We did not include letters,[174] SMS texts reproduced in the papers, or short trails for articles later in the paper. We did not assess where in the paper these articles appeared (for example, as a front-page splash), the headlines or photos used to accompany them, the length of the article, or where in the article the sceptical voice or voices appeared. The search options often came up with several repeats which we removed from the sample. The 'at the start' option also reduced the number of articles which would have appeared if we had used the 'anywhere in the text' option, although, as we shall see, the sample size was usually sufficiently robust for each of the periods and for each of the papers. This is largely because we did not, as is the usual practice with media academics, reduce the sample by random selection. We also did not distinguish between the daily and Sunday editions of newspapers.

The text of the coding sheets can be seen in Appendix 2. We first measured the total number of articles with mentions of 'climate change' or 'global warming' near the start, and then the number where sceptical voices were present (section 3). We then divided the latter into the six different classes of articles as in the paragraph above (section 4). The next section assessed the different ways the sceptical voices appeared in news reports, features and reviews (section 5a). This included what turned out to be a large category of generic quoting of sceptics, where individuals are not named but phrases such as 'sceptics say that' were included. The following section (section 5b) assessed the different ways such voices appeared in opinion pieces, and the next one the nature of the editorials where sceptical voices were discussed (section 5c).

The following two sections (sections 6 and 7) listed the names of individual sceptics where they were directly or indirectly quoted in the news reports (rather than simply being mentioned), and then the names of those who authored sceptical opinion pieces as invited columnists or who were quoted or briefly described in the opinion pieces of regular columnists writing on the newspapers (but not in editorials).[175] A total was given for the number of times these sceptics appeared (not for the number of sceptics – often the same sceptic was mentioned or quoted several times in the same period). These names were then assigned in section 8 to different types of scepticism broadly along the three categories of (i) those who say global temperatures are not warming, (ii) those who say they are warming, but argue that the anthropogenic contribution to global warming or climate change is

---

[174] This is to be regretted as an analysis of the presence of letters expressing a sceptical view could have provided a helpful insight both into the nature of the readership of a particular newspaper, or perhaps the editorial preferences of that paper. Impressionistic evidence would suggest a heavy preponderance of letters from sceptical readers of the right-leaning press, although this would have to be verified.
[175] As it turned out, they were only a handful of mentions in the news reports – see row 13 in Table 4.1.

over-stated, negligible, or non-existent compared to other factors like natural variations or sun spots, and (iii) those who those who accept it is happening but for different reasons question its impacts or the need to do something about it.

Finally, we classified each of the named sceptics according to their main professional background or affiliation (section 9). There were nine categories: university scientist (e.g. Richard Lindzen), an academic tied to university but not a scientist (e.g. Bjørn Lomborg), a non-university-based research organisation (e.g. NASA), a think tank or lobbying group (e.g. the Global Warming Policy Foundation in the UK), an 'amateur' scientist with no affiliation to the previous four options (e.g. Steve McIntyre[176]), a newspaper columnist or media personality (e.g. Rush Limbaugh in the USA), a politician or diplomat (e.g. James Inhofe), the business sector, and 'other'.

In each of the five country coding sheets other than the UK, the articles where sceptics were mentioned were double-checked by the lead author to assess whether the coding was consistently applied across all six countries, and changed where appropriate.[177] Several important issues arose out of the application of the methodology which are discussed fully in Appendix 3. The advantages and weaknesses of the methodology are also explained there.

The results

Table 4.1 shows the results taken from the coding sheets for the two print media in each of the six countries. Row 1 gives the number of articles mentioning 'climate change' or 'global warming' near or at the start. The total number of articles analysed was 3,327. The UK had the most at 941, followed by Brazil (873) and India (649). This is not surprising given the high interest in the UK media in 'Climategate', which was partly due to the fact the University of East Anglia is situated in the UK. The high volume of coverage of global warming in the media in Brazil and India fits a general picture found in other surveys.[178] China had the least coverage at 152 articles. The *Guardian* had the greatest number of articles (554) followed by *Folha* (473), *Estado* (400), and the *Times of India* (389). In all 12 newspapers, the volume of coverage increased between period 1 and 2.

Row 2 shows the number of articles for each newspaper and period in which sceptics are 'mentioned'. It is important to explain what 'mentioning sceptics' means: it includes direct and indirect quotes, short mentions, generic quotes, opinion pieces, and editorials (see rows 4 to 9 of Table 4.1) The *Telegraph* in the UK had the most with 74 articles, followed by the *Guardian* with 61. The two Chinese newspapers

---

[176] We do not mean 'amateur' in any derogatory sense, but rather as a description of the absence of any affiliation to a university or research institute.

[177] We did not apply inter-coder reliability tests, but we did check that the different sections of the coding sheets were applied in the same manner across all six countries.

[178] Painter, *Summoned by Science*, 44, and UN DPI report (n. 154 above), 9.

	Estado 1	Estado 2	Folha 1	Folha 2	Peoples Daily 1	Peoples Daily 2	B Evening News 1	B Evening News 2
1. Number of articles in sample	184	216	212	261	21	87	17	27
2. Mentioning sceptics	1	7	2	7	2	5	2	3
3. Percentage	1	3	1	3	10	6	12	11
Where did articles quoting sceptics appear?								
4. News reports	1	3	1	3	0	1	2	3
5. Features	0	0	0	0	0	0	0	0
6. Opinion pieces	0	4	1	4	2	4	0	0
7. Editorials	0	0	0	0	0	0	0	0
8. Reviews	0	0	0	0	0	0	0	0
9. Other	0	0	0	0	0	0	0	0
Main way sceptical voices included in 4,5,8,9								
10. Direct quotes	1	0	1	0	0	1	0	0
11. Indirect quotes	0	0	0	0	0	0	0	0
12. Generic	0	1	0	1	0	0	0	3
13. Mentioned, not quoted	0	2	0	2	0	0	0	0
14. Vox Pops	0	0	0	0	0	0	0	0
15. Other	0	0	0	0	0	0	2	0
Main way sceptical voices included in opinion pieces								
16. Author as sceptical scientist	0	0	0	1	0	0	0	0
17. Regular columnist expressing sceptical view	0	0	0	2	0	0	0	0
18. Invited columnist other than scientist	0	0	0	0	0	0	0	0
19. Sceptical voices included but contested	0	4	1	1	2	4	0	0
Main way sceptical voices included in editorials								
20. Consensus view seriously contested	0	0	0	0	0	0	0	0
21. Tone generally sceptical of measures	0	0	0	0	0	0	0	0
22. Sceptical views included but contested	0	0	0	0	0	0	0	0
23. Number of times sceptics appearing in 10 and 11	1	0	1	0	0	1	0	0
24. Number of times sceptics appearing in 16-19	0	0	0	3	0	0	0	0
Types of sceptic								
25. Deny global temperatures are warming	0	0	0	0	0	0	0	0
26. Anthropogenic contribution over-stated or negligible	1	0	1	1	0	1	0	0
27. Serious doubts about impacts or need to combat	0	0	0	2	0	0	0	0
28. Science or findings of IPCC seriously flawed	0	0	0	0	0	0	0	0
Professional background to sceptics								
29. University scientist	0	0	1	2	0	1	0	0
30. Other academic	0	0	0	1	0	0	0	0
31. Research group	0	0	0	0	0	0	0	0
32. Think tank	0	0	0	0	0	0	0	0
33. Amateur	0	0	0	0	0	0	0	0
34. Columnist/media	0	0	0	0	0	0	0	0
35. Politician/diplomat	1	0	0	0	0	0	0	0
36. Business	0	0	0	0	0	0	0	0
37. Other	0	0	0	0	0	0	0	0

Table 4.1. Prevalence of sceptical voices in six countries' print media, 2007 and 2009/10

Le Figaro 1	Le Figaro 2	Le Monde 1	Le Monde 2	Times of India 1	Times of India 2	The Hindu 1	The Hindu 2	Guardian/Obs 1	Guardian/Obs 2	Telegraph 1	Telegraph 2	NYT 1	NYT 2	WSJ 1	WSJ 2	Totals
58	60	71	136	93	296	32	228	241	313	149	238	116	112	69	90	3,327
3	4	8	7	7	16	1	17	10	51	19	55	24	32	9	36	328
5	7	11	5	8	4	3	8	4	16	13	23	21	29	13	40	10
0	1	3	1	6	10	1	13	5	35	5	26	12	20	3	13	168
2	1	2	3	0	0	0	0	1	0	2	2	0	0	0	0	13
1	2	2	1	1	5	0	4	3	11	10	24	6	8	2	15	110
0	0	1	1	0	1	0	0	0	4	1	3	6	4	4	8	33
0	0	0	1	0	0	0	0	1	1	1	0	0	0	0	0	4
0	0	0	0	0	0	0	0	0	0	0	0	0	0	0	0	0
1	1	1	0	1	8	0	6	1	15	7	18	9	11	2	4	88
0	0	3	1	1	0	0	0	6	4	0	3	1	0	0	3	22
0	1	0	0	3	2	1	7	0	15	1	6	0	9	0	6	56
0	0	0	1	0	0	0	0	0	2	0	1	0	0	0	0	8
0	0	0	0	0	0	0	0	0	0	0	0	1	0	1	0	2
1	0	1	3	1	0	0	0	0	0	0	0	1	0	0	0	9
0	0	0	0	0	0	0	0	0	0	2	0	0	0	1	1	5
0	1	0	0	0	3	0	0	0	0	2	13	0	0	1	6	28
1	1	0	0	1	0	0	1	0	2	2	0	0	0	0	7	15
0	0	2	1	0	2	0	3	3	9	4	11	6	8	0	1	62
0	0	0	0	0	0	0	0	0	0	0	0	0	0	2	5	7
0	0	0	0	0	0	0	0	0	0	0	0	0	0	2	2	4
0	0	1	1	0	1	0	0	0	4	1	3	6	4	0	1	22
3	1	7	2	5	11	0	3	10	48	12	28	22	16	3	8	182
1	2	2	1	1	2	0	4	4	12	10	20	1	3	2	10	78
0	1	0	0	0	1	0	0	0	2	0	0	4	8	1	3	20
4	2	9	3	5	11	0	7	13	36	19	27	7	8	3	6	164
0	0	0	0	1	1	0	0	1	22	3	21	9	3	1	9	73
0	0	0	0	0	0	0	0	0	0	0	0	3	0	0	0	3
2	0	5	0	4	2	0	3	4	4	9	4	8	2	1	3	55
0	0	0	0	2	1	0	0	0	7	0	4	2	2	0	5	24
0	0	0	0	0	3	0	0	3	0	5	1	0	0	1	1	14
0	0	0	0	0	2	0	0	0	9	2	3	1	1	1	2	21
1	0	0	0	0	2	0	2	3	12	2	9	0	0	0	1	32
0	1	0	0	0	1	0	0	1	2	1	1	0	2	0	0	9
1	2	2	2	0	2	0	2	2	23	2	26	5	11	1	6	88
0	0	2	1	0	0	0	0	1	1	1	0	3	0	0	0	9
0	0	0	0	0	0	0	0	0	2	0	0	4	1	1	0	8

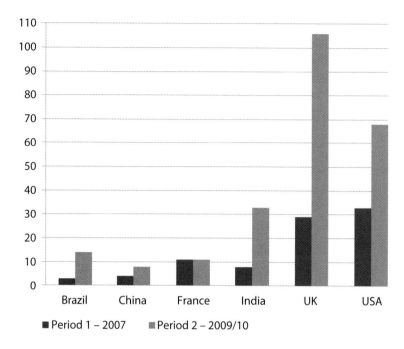

■ Period 1 – 2007   ■ Period 2 – 2009/10

Figure 4.2. Number of Articles Containing Sceptical Voices in Six Countries, 2007 and 2009/10

had the least. Figure 4.2 gives the breakdown by country. It shows the sharp contrast between the USA and the UK on the one hand, and the remaining four countries.

Row 3 shows the number of articles with mentions of sceptics as a percentage of the total number of articles covering climate change or global warming. This is a better measure of the prevalence of sceptics than counting the absolute numbers of articles, partly because we did not make any adjustment for the total news 'hole' available for articles on climate change in each of the newspapers examined. In other words, *The Hindu* for example would have had far less space available (24–8 pages on a weekday) for articles about climate change than the *New York Times* (100 pages plus).

In the first period, the range was between 1% (*Estado, Folha*) and 13% (*Daily Telegraph, Wall Street Journal*). In the second it was between 3% (*Estado, Folha*) and 40% (*Wall Street Journal*). In eight of the newspapers, the percentage increased between the two periods, most notably in the *Wall Street Journal* from 9 to 40%. In four cases, it dropped (in the two Chinese newspapers, *Le Figaro* and the *Times of India*).

Perhaps the most significant result is the comparison between countries. In Brazil the range was between 1 and 3% of articles over the two periods, the lowest of all the six countries. The next lowest was India, between 3 and 8%, followed by France (5 to 11%). China was next, with a range of 6 to 12%, although the relatively high figures for the first

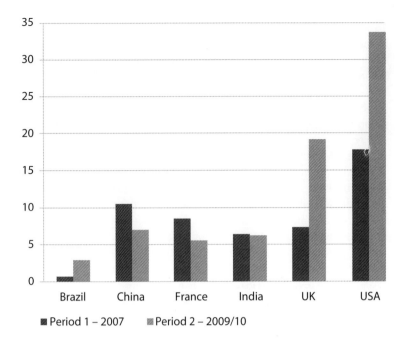

■ Period 1 – 2007   ▩ Period 2 – 2009/10

Figure 4.3. Articles Containing Sceptical Voices as % of Total Number of Articles in Six Countries, 2007 and 2009/10

period of sampling were taken from a low base. The two countries with the highest range were the UK with 4 to 23%, and the USA which had the highest at between 13 and 40%. Figure 4.3 shows the breakdown by country, and highlights again the sharp contrast between the USA and the UK compared to the other countries, particularly in the second period. In the first period, the UK emerges with a lower percentage than China and France, mainly because the *Guardian* had few mentions of sceptics. However, the *Telegraph* had the highest percentage of any newspaper outside the USA (at 13%).

In the USA and the UK, over the two periods the left-leaning newspaper had a lower percentage of articles with sceptics in them than the more right-leaning newspaper. This tendency is explored further with the larger sample in the UK outlined in Chapter 6, where the tendency is more marked. In Brazil, there was no difference between the two papers, and in France and India there was virtually no difference: *Le Monde* had a slightly higher percentage of articles with sceptics in them over the two periods (7%) than *Le Figaro* (6%). And in the case of India, the percentage figures were 6% for the *Times of India*, and 7% for *The Hindu* (although as discussed above, the *Times of India* is more centrist than right-leaning).

Rows 4–9 show in what type of articles the sceptical voices appeared. In Brazil, China, India, and France, there are only a handful of opinion pieces or editorials where sceptical voices are quoted or mentioned.

These will be discussed in the country-specific sections below. However, in the UK and US press, articles in the opinion pages and editorial pages mentioning sceptics figure quite prominently: 15 in the *Guardian* in the second period, 11 then 27 in the *Telegraph*, 12 each in the two periods in the *NYT*, and 23 in the second period in the *WSJ*. Opinion pieces represented a significant percentage of the overall number of articles mentioning sceptics in these four newspapers: 29% in the *Guardian* in the second period, 58% then 49% in the *Telegraph*, 50% then 38% in the *NYT*, and 64% in the *WSJ* in the second period.

It is also interesting to see in which parts of a newspaper mentions of sceptical voices are most likely to be found. Brazil, China, France, and India probably have too small a sample to draw any conclusions. But in the UK and the USA, over the two periods a higher percentage of articles with sceptical voices is found in the news pages of the left-leaning press (*Guardian/Observer, NYT*) than in the combined total of opinion pages and the editorials. For the right-leaning-press (*Telegraph/WSJ*), it is the reverse. (See Table 4.2.)

Table 4.2. Articles Containing Sceptical Voices by Type of Article, UK and US Newspapers, 2007 and 2009/10 (%)

	Guard/Obs	Telegraph	NYT	WSJ
News reports, features, reviews	70	49	57	36
Opinion pieces, editorials	30	51	43	64

However, perhaps the more meaningful test is *how* sceptical voices appeared in the opinion pieces and editorials. The *Guardian/Observer* had 11 opinion pieces in period 2 which quoted or briefly described sceptics, but 9 of them were essentially dismissive of sceptical views. The two others were by Benny Peiser and Bjørn Lomborg, but their pieces appeared as a part of a wider sequence of opinion pieces. In contrast, the *Daily/Sunday Telegraph* included 24 opinion pieces over the same period of which over half (13) were by regular columnists (9 authored by Christopher Booker in the *Sunday Telegraph*) expressing an essentially sceptical viewpoint. In the first period, the *Telegraphs* included 10 opinion pieces of which 6 were sceptical. Likewise, the *NYT* ran 8 opinion pieces in the second period, all of which were dismissive of sceptical viewpoints, whilst the *WSJ* ran 15 of which only one was dismissive. (See Chapter 5 for more discussion of this point.)

Rows 20–22 show that Brazil, China, France, and India only ran three editorials mentioning sceptical voices across the two research periods, all of which were essentially to dismiss the sceptical viewpoint. The *Guardian* and *Telegraph* ran 4 each, and the *NYT* 10 – all 18 were essentially dismissive. In contrast the *WSJ* ran 12, only one of which was dismissive of the sceptical arguments. Table 4.3 shows the sharp contrast within the USA and the UK between the left-leaning and right-leaning newspaper in each country.[179]

Table 4.3 Articles, Opinion Pieces, and Editorials Containing Sceptical Voices in Left- and Right-Leaning Newspapers in the UK and USA, 2007 and 2009/10

	UK		USA	
	Guardian	Telegraph	New York Times	Wall Street Journal
No. of articles mentioning sceptics	61	74	56	45
No. of these as a % of all climate change articles	11	19	25	28
No. of opinion pieces mentioning sceptics	14	34	14	17
% of these in which sceptical views are not contested	0	56	0	94
No. of editorials mentioning sceptics	4	4	10	12
% of these in which sceptical views are not contested	0	0	0	92

Rows 23–24 of Table 4.1 show the number of times named sceptics were quoted or mentioned. The *Guardian* in the second period had the most at 60, but this was to a large extent driven by its decision to publish a series of in-depth articles by Fred Pearce in early February 2010. (See discussion in Chapter 6.) In the same period, the *Telegraphs* came next with 48, followed by the *NYT* (19) and the *WSJ* (18). It is interesting to note that of the 18 in the *WSJ*, 10 were quoted or described in opinion pieces. Of the non-Anglo-Saxon countries, the *Times of India* had the most at 13 (second period) followed by *Le Monde* with 9 (in the first period), but in general the figures were sharply lower than in the UK and US newspapers.

Rows 25–28 divide the sceptics into the different categories described in fuller detail on the coding sheet. Of the 260 times they were mentioned, 20 of them were 'type 1' sceptics (outright deniers that global temperatures are warming) – most of these were quotes from, or descriptions of, the Republican senator in the USA, James Inhofe, who is known to have espoused this view. 164 of these were quotes or mentions from the 'stronger' type of sceptics who question the anthropogenic contribution (equivalent to 63%), more than twice the 73 (or 28%) from those who accept it is happening but for different reasons question its impacts or the need to do something about it.

Finally, rows 29–37 give the professional background or affiliation of the sceptics. The largest category was politicians or diplomats (88

---

[179] We have classified the two opinion pieces by Peiser and Lomborg in the *Guardian* as 'contested' for the purposes of Table 4.3 as, although they were not contested within the article, they were contested by other articles in the sequence. This explains the discrepancy with row 18 of Table 4.1.

times or 34%), followed by university climate scientists (55 or 21%) and 'amateurs' (32 times or 12%). Next came other academics (9%), lobby groups (8%), research groups (5%), columnists and other media (3%), business (3%), and other (3%). Another way of expressing this is that sceptical voices who were not scientists attached to a university represented nearly 80% of all the sceptical voices mentioned.

The four newspapers in the USA and the UK accounted for 76 of the 88 times politicians were mentioned, equivalent to 86%. The two US newspapers accounted for 23 times and the UK 53 times, which were swollen by the high presence of Lord Lawson of the GWPF (23 times). It is interesting to note that, in the USA, politicians represented 35% of all sceptics, the largest category by some margin. They were also the largest category in the UK (37%). The Chinese newspapers quoted or mentioned no politicians, the Brazilians one (Joe Barton from the USA), the French two national (Claude Allègre and Jean-Marie Le Pen) and two foreign, and the Indians no national and four foreign.

It is also interesting to note that in the two UK print media, the number of times representatives of lobby groups were quoted or mentioned increased from 2 to 12 between periods 1 and 2. If Lord Lawson from the GWPF had been assigned to this category (instead of that of a politician), the figure would have been much higher. Likewise, in the UK media, the number of times 'amateur' sceptics were mentioned went up from 5 to 21 over the two periods, largely due to the coverage of 'Climategate'. We shall discuss this theme further in Chapter 6.

Summary

So how can we best summarise the answers to our six research questions posed at the beginning of this chapter? First, as you would expect, the number of articles with sceptical voices within them increased for all the print media and countries included in our survey between the two periods, with the exception of *Le Monde*. However, whereas the absolute number of articles may have increased in virtually all media in the six countries, there were important differences between them: the percentage of those articles with sceptical voices in them increased significantly in the case of the *Guardian, Telegraph, NYT,* and *WSJ* (a percentage increase of between 8 and 27%), mildly in the case of *Folha, Estado, Le Figaro*, and *The Hindu* (an increase of between 2 and 5%) and actually dropped in the case of the two Chinese newspapers, the *Times of India*, and *Le Monde*.

Such results are perhaps not surprising given that the UK and US media paid much more attention to 'Climategate' and the controversies around the IPCC reports, which fell within the second period of study. As we have already mentioned, it would have been very difficult to cover these topics adequately without the extensive quoting of sceptical voices. A different selection of the second period might have revealed different results for some countries, as we shall discuss in Chapter 5. A further period of research after the furore abated could have revealed whether their presence was sustained. A limited survey of three months' coverage in 2010 of the *FT* and *Telegraphs* in the UK does suggest that the number of articles dropped considerably after our second period of analysis, but that the percentage with sceptical voices actually increased (see Chapter 6).

Secondly, there are very significant differences between the six countries in the amount of sceptical voices quoted or mentioned. Expressed simply, the UK and the US media in the survey mentioned or quoted significantly more sceptics than the French, Brazilian, Indian, and Chinese media. In part, this was due to the coverage (or lack of it) of 'Climategate' and the IPCC controversies, but there were several other interesting factors which explain the country differences. These will be explored in the following chapter, but they include journalistic norms and cultures in each country, the presence or not of organised or vocal climate scepticism amongst scientists, lobby groups, politicians and NGOs, the influence of newspaper proprietors and editors over output, and the readership target of individual newspapers.

Thirdly, there is strong evidence for thinking that in the countries where sceptical voices appear in greater numbers, they are more likely to be found in right-leaning than left-leaning print media. There are important country variations. In China, left/right splits are not relevant. In Brazil, France, and India, where few sceptic voices appear, there was little or no difference in the prevalence of sceptical viewpoints between the two print media chosen. However, in the case of the UK and the USA, there is a clear statistical difference between the right- and left-leaning newspapers. In the UK, the left-leaning *Guardian* had fewer articles with sceptical voices than the right-leaning *Telegraph* in each of the two periods (despite the former's extensive coverage of 'Climategate'). In the USA, the *NYT* had more in the first period than the *WSJ*, but over the two periods it had slightly less (25% compared to 28%). It would seem that in these Anglophone countries, the perspective of a newspaper appears to play a role.

But counting the number of sceptical voices of course does not capture *how* they were quoted. Virtually all of the sceptical voices quoted or described in the *Guardian*'s opinion pages, for example, were included to be later refuted. As discussed above, the *Telegraph* and *WSJ* had considerably more uncontested sceptical opinion pieces and/ or editorials than the *Guardian* and *NYT*. The difference in the USA is particularly marked as the *NYT* ran 10 editorials over the two periods, all of which were dismissive of sceptic arguments, whereas the *WSJ* ran 12, only one of which seemed to be dismissive. In France, *Le Monde* only mentioned or quoted sceptics to reject their views. Nor did it give space to sceptics in either period in its opinion pieces. In contrast, *Le Figaro* did – on three occasions – give space to them in its opinion pieces. The more marked differences between right- and left-leaning papers that emerge from the wider UK study will be discussed in Chapter 6, and a wider discussion of the possible drivers behind it.

Fourthly, of all the 328 articles across the six countries in which sceptical voices were found, 181 of these were in the news pages (55%), and 143 were opinion pieces or editorials (43%). This latter figure is probably higher than many would expect. Again, there are significant country variations: Brazil, China, India, and France have many fewer editorials or opinion pieces where such voices are found. Collectively the eight newspapers there account for 34 such pieces in our sample (24% of the total). There is also evidence that such pieces occupy a greater percentage of the total number of articles in the right-leaning press in the UK and US (*Telegraph* and *WSJ*) than in the left-leaning press (*Guardian* and *NYT*).

Fifthly, there were more than twice the numbers of mentions of type (ii) sceptics who question the anthropogenic contribution than the number of those who accept it is happening but for different reasons question its impacts or the need to do something about it. It is interesting to note that type (ii) sceptics were much more common in the print media in Brazil, China, India, and France, representing 45 out of the 51 times sceptics were quoted or mentioned, or 88%. In the Anglo-Saxon countries, for type (ii) sceptics, the percentage figure was lower (57%). Of the 73 times type (iii) sceptics were quoted or mentioned in all six countries, only four were in the non-Anglo-Saxon media. It was a particular phenomenon of the UK print media that sceptics from outside the country received considerable attention, whereas in France, Brazil, India, and China it is the (reduced number of) sceptics in their own countries who are predominately quoted or given space.

Finally, university climate scientists represented 21% of all the sceptics quoted or mentioned in the total sample, compared to the most represented group of politicians and diplomats (34%). It is highly significant that the UK and US print media accounted for the vast majority of the times that this latter group were quoted or included (86%). Politicians were the largest single category of sceptics quoted in these two countries. France was the only other country to quote national politicians (five times), whilst of the other three countries China quoted no politician at all, and India and Brazil only foreigners.

5. Country Studies

Brazil

Carlos Henrique Fioravanti and James Painter

Context

We chose two of the most influential newspapers in Brazil for inclusion in our survey. In 2010, *Folha de São Paulo*, the largest daily newspaper in the country, sold between 280,000 and 330,000 copies every day. Even though it is based in São Paulo, it has a national circulation. It is left of centre, whereas its main rival and São Paulo's second largest newspaper, *O Estado de São Paulo* is right of centre. In 2010 *Estado* had a circulation of around 280,000 on Sundays and 210,000 on weekdays. Both papers target an audience from the upper socio-economic groups.

There is some evidence for thinking that coverage of global warming and climate change in the Brazilian print media began to take off in the latter half of 2006.[180] Recent studies suggest that Brazil enjoyed the highest amount of media coverage of the 2009 Copenhagen summit of any country in the world. This was in part due to the large number of Brazilian journalists there – it had the second largest contingent (100) of any developing country after China (which had slightly more at 103).[181] There are several reasons for this high turnout, but one of them is that many of Brazil's main newspapers and magazines have dedicated teams of science and environment editors, correspondents, or reporters. TV Globo, which by repute is the largest privately owned TV station in the world and dominates the domestic media scene, regularly covers climate change issues, whilst the country's largest economic newspaper, *Valor Economico*, has a dedicated environment correspondent.

An indication of how much importance *Estado* has given to environment issues in the last few years is shown by the creation of *Vida&* in 2004, followed by the start of a monthly supplement *Planeta*

---

[180] ANDI, 'Climate Change in the Brazilian Press: A Comparative Analysis of 50 Newspapers from July 2005 to June 2007, July 2007 to December 2008', and Painter, *Summoned by Science*, 18 n. 32.
[181] Painter, *Summoned by Science*, 44 and 106.

e Sustentatibilidade in 2009. In 2010 *Planeta* became a daily section and a weekly page in addition to being a monthly supplement. The *Estado* group has contracted more specialised reporters to cover the expansion of environment issues across its different media outlets.

Folha started training a lot of scientist reporters from 2000 onwards to work for their science desk which was particularly influential inside and outside the paper. The two editors from 2000 to 2010 were science specialists who had both studied journalism abroad.

Prior to 'Climategate', there was very little tradition of climate scepticism in the media. US media academic Myanna Lahsen who lives in Brazil says that 'climate scepticism is hardly existent in the Brazilian media. There are only a few dissident voices, and they are rarely featured. There are occasional articles about foreign (US and UK) contrarians, but also few on that front.'[182]

Partly, this is because of the absence of well-organised and funded lobby groups linked to the fossil fuel or extractive industries as found in the USA or Australia. In Brazil, electricity is 80% hydropower-generated, and until recently the oil industry was a state monopoly. There is also considerable business and political clout behind the country's much-heralded biofuels programme. Logging interests in the Amazon are mostly illegal, and those that are legally registered may be trading with illegally forested timber. So logging companies keep a low profile and would not contest climate change legislation as they depend on government licences to exploit new areas. All this has meant that there has been little political or ideological space for right-wing think tanks feeding sceptical arguments.

Another factor is that much of the coverage of science in the Brazilian media is driven by scientific papers appearing in Brazilian and international journals, where there is little space afforded to sceptical arguments.[183] A few well-known Brazilian climatologists like Jose Marengo and the Nobre brothers (Carlos and Antonio) are given ample space in the media and are well-respected there. Carlos Nobre was a lead author of the IPCC 2007 reports, and currently is National Secretary of the Brazilian Ministry of Science and Technology.

Brazilian journalists interviewed for this study also emphasised the strong journalistic culture of science and environment reporting which carried considerable weight within newspapers and other media outlets, and strongly influenced their editorial line on climate scepticism. For example, Claudio Angelo, a former science editor at *Folha*, remembered his former boss, Marcelo Leite, who created *Folha*'s science desk, telling him back in 2000 that the American press made a 'mistake' 10 years ago by treating sceptics like a mandatory 'other side' to climate stories, and that *Folha*'s science desk did not need to do the same.

Finally, 'Climategate' did make some waves in the Brazilian media, but to nothing like the extent it did in the UK and US press. One journalist

---

[182] Correspondence with author by email, May 2011.
[183] Carlos Fioravanti, a former RISJ fellow, has written a paper suggesting ways of reducing the dependency on scientific papers. See http://jcom.sissa.it/archive/09/04/Jcom0904(2010)A02.

interviewed could not remember it making a headline piece, in part because it was felt to be happening a long way away for many Brazilian readers, and because it was a complicated story to explain. Claudio Angelo said that he felt

> *Folha underreported 'Climategate', partly to resist the media frenzy created in the UK around the affair, and partly because Brazil has never hyped climate change the way the British press did, with a lot of doom-and-gloom stories. The British media overreacted both ways; by giving undue apocalyptic coverage to the IPCC reports in 2007 and by giving undue time to anti-science viewpoints after 'Climategate'.*

Results

Given the above, it is perhaps to be expected that the two Brazilian newspapers showed the lowest percentage of articles quoting sceptics of any of the 20 newspapers included in this survey, in both periods. (See Table 4.1, columns 1-4 for the full figures.) Despite the fact that Brazil had one of the largest samples of newspapers articles included in each period, the number of articles mentioning sceptics ranged between only 1 and 7. Other points to emerge are:

- There is very little difference between the left-leaning and right-leaning paper in terms of the number of articles quoting sceptics over the two periods (1 or 2 then 7 in both newspapers), and the percentage they represent (1% then 3%).

- Both newspapers had four opinion pieces quoting sceptics, although in the case of *Folha*, three of the four were in some sense 'sceptical'.

- In the case of *Estado*, the number of sceptical voices quoted actually dropped from one to zero between the two periods, despite 'Climategate' (see rows 23 and 24). In *Folha*, it went up slightly from one to three.

- It is interesting to note that of the five sceptics who were quoted in both newspapers over both periods, four of them were scientists or experts attached to Brazilian universities or research centres. The exception was one quote from Joe Barton, a Republican congressman in the USA, who was quoted in *Estado* from a report by the news agency EFE. There were none from lobby groups.

Discussion

Results from questionnaires received back from an editor and journalist from each of the two newspapers would corroborate some of the findings. In the case of *Estado*, it is clear that 'Climategate' did make an impact on its readers, journalists, and editors, but did not necessarily lead to more sceptics being quoted. As Afra Balazina, an environment reporter on the paper, described it, 'we had to explain that (such things) were caused by a small group, the sceptics, and that there were more than a thousand scientists in the IPCC'. She describes the sceptics as a 'minority', and 'not the other side, as they are not a representative group. They are not reliable for us to give them space.' It is a view broadly echoed by Luciana Monte Constantino, the executive editor of the paper, who said 'we have a balanced approach. Sceptics have had less space because they are not representative and don't always have a scientific argument.' Both respondents confirmed that the sceptical voices are more likely to be heard in opinion pieces than in news articles.

A slightly different picture emerges from *Folha*, where the two respondents both said that during 2010 the paper did give more space to sceptics, although this had, according to one, dropped off in 2011. Both said that these voices were to be found in the opinion pieces, which would be in line with our findings. Marcelo Leite, a former science editor at the paper, and now the opinion editor, said there had been positive aspects from 'Climategate' in that prior to 2010/11 'there was a Manichaeism, as if all the IPCC did was good and scientists were always right. It was good to puncture the unanimity.' He and Reinaldo José Lopes, the current science editor, both said that the paper valued plurality of opinions and, in the words of Leite, 'a predisposition' rather than pressure from editors or owners at the newspaper to include more sceptical voices, and 'an automatic attitude to publish different views in the face of unanimity'.

Finally, all four of the respondents said they personally did not share the views of sceptics in the senses used in this study, although two of them mentioned how climate modelling needs to be improved and, according to Leite, better explained and described. All four also said they had not been lobbied by organised sceptical groups (although in some cases individual sceptics had made their case).

As mentioned above, virtually the only difference to emerge from our survey between the two papers was that *Folha* gave space to four sceptics in their opinion pieces, particularly in the second period. These were all Brazilian: Gustavo Baptista, Cesar Benjamin, and José Carlos Almeida Azevedo appeared in December 2009 and January 2010. Baptista is the author of a book called *Global Warming: Science or Religion?*, and an assistant professor at the University of Brasilia, while Cesar Benjamin is a social scientist and regular columnist. Azevedo (now deceased) was a military man who was dean at the University of Brasilia, and adopted climate scepticism after retirement. He appeared in the opinion pages of *Folha* several times. He is regarded by journalists interviewed for this study as one of Brazil's two 'serious' climate sceptics with a background in physical sciences. The other is the meteorologist Luiz Carlos Molion, a member of the World Meteorological Organization, and director of the Institute of Atmospheric Sciences at the Federal University of Alagoas. His scepticism about the human causes of global warming was reported, for example, in *Folha* on 15 March 2008, outside the period of our research.

In the first period, *Folha* also gave space to Aziz Ab'Saber, an elderly and widely respected geographer and emeritus professor at the University of São Paulo, but someone who is not regarded as a prominent or vocal sceptic. In contrast to the four Brazilians given space in *Folha*, the only 'sceptic' quoted in *Estado* came from abroad – as already mentioned, the Republican senator in the USA, Joe Barton.[184]

It is also worth pointing out that in neither of the papers were there any quotes from Brazilian sceptical politicians or businessmen, which is in sharp contrast to the situation in the UK and US media. This reflects the dominant political and business culture in Brazil, where there is no strongly vocal presence of sceptics in either sector. All mainstream political parties accept the need to combat climate change, and there was little sustained political opposition to ex-President Lula's passing into law in December 2009 the setting of ambitious voluntary targets for cuts in GHG emissions by 2020.[185] Many of Brazil's business elite belong to the powerful agriculture export sector, some of whom are concerned about what is happening, and will happen, to the Amazon's and the country's climate as a result of global warming. Other sectors stand to gain from the continued pursuit of ambitious plans to further biofuel production, where Brazil is second only to the USA in volume of output. Petrobras, the giant Brazilian oil company, is state-owned. It has no clear, public position about climate change, but it does have multiple interests including investment in companies which produce the biofuel ethanol. Petrobras and other extractive industries would only be affected if the voluntary targets are rigorously implemented.

In summary then, climate scepticism is hardly present in the Brazilian media, although it may have increased a little, particularly in the opinion columns of *Folha*, in the period after 'Climategate' and the IPCC controversies. At least in our survey, there was little variation between the left-leaning and right-leaning newspapers. The reasons for this are multiple, but journalistic culture, the absence of organised

---

[184] In an article on 18 Mar. 2007 two professors from the UK (Paul Hardaker and Chris Collier from the Royal Meteorological Society) were quoted in another article based on an EFE report. They were excluded from our sample because, although they were critical of some researchers making claims about possible future impacts that cannot be justified by the science, they essentially believe in the human causes of global warming and the potential dangers of it. See http://news.bbc.co.uk/1/hi/6460635.stm.
[185] Aldo Rebelo, a deputy for the Communist party, is a recent exception. He has campaigned for a new Forest Code on the ground that it would help small farmers, but critics say this would allow more development of the Amazon and threaten Brazil's ambitious targets to cut GHGs. Rebelo has said that he is sceptical of climate change and does not believe in the 'theory of global warming'.

lobby groups linked to the fossil fuel industry, and the virtual absence of strongly sceptical voices in the elite scientific, political, and business community have all played a role.

China

by Rebecca Nadin and James Painter

Climate scepticism with Chinese characteristics

Climate scepticism in China is not on the same scale as in some Western countries. In China, unlike in the West, there is no public division between those who accept or reject climate science. It is rare to hear Chinese academics, officials, or the public deny climate change or declare they do not believe in the science of climate change. Historically, scientific knowledge and accomplishment has been highly regarded and trusted in Chinese society. Similarly, climate change has not become as politically contentious an issue domestically in China as it has in some other countries. This in part is due to the one-party political system and because domestic climate change mitigation policies fit within the government's own objectives around energy security and efficiency. In government pronouncements there is no questioning of the core link between GHG emissions and atmospheric warming.

Rather than focusing on the anthropogenic contribution debate, 'climate scepticism with Chinese characteristics' centres on certain aspects of the IPCC findings, in particular the speed and severity of climate change, and on the motivations of developed countries for seeking a legally binding agreement.[186] Amongst government officials and scholars there is scepticism about the scientific case for keeping global temperature rises to less than 2°C and how much change in temperature is dangerous. There is also a prominent discourse on the possible positive impacts of climate change for China. Following 'Climategate', Chinese academics became more confident in challenging the Western consensus on climate science. As already mentioned in Chapter 3, chief negotiator Xie Zhenhua told reporters in early 2010 that China intended to keep 'an open mind on global warming'. Others took the opportunity to question the authority of the IPCC and the under-representation of the developing world in panels assessing the science.[187]

However, there are some influential and well-quoted academics and advisers who are more extreme in their scepticism. Both Cheng Jicheng

[186] R. L. Nadin and P. Willats, 'Framing Climate Change: Social and Political Discourses, a China Case Study', unpublished manuscript, 2011.
[187] As a member of the IPCC, the former China Meteorological Administration Chairman Qin Dahe shared the 2007 Peace Prize with Al Gore. However, Chinese academics accounted for less than 2% of contributors to the IPCC AR4 report.

and Li Qi, who are Professors of Digital Earth Sciences at Peking University, have publicly proclaimed their doubts about global warming and released a report questioning claims made by the IPCC.[188] Ding Zhongli, Vice-President of the Chinese Academy of Sciences, believes that the IPCC overemphasises the impact that carbon emissions have on temperature.[189] Zhu Kezhen, a well-known Chinese meteorologist, believes that climate change is merely a natural occurrence and points out that sun activity could be the main driver of climate fluctuations. Scepticism of certain scientific findings is not limited to earth scientists and meteorologists. Gou Hongyang, a market analyst, argues in his book *Low-Carbon Plot* that developed countries are using carbon emissions as an excuse to hinder the economic progress of developing countries.[190] This theme is also picked up by Xie Zhenghui, a professor at the Institute of Atmospheric Physics, Chinese Academy of Sciences, who believes that temperature increases would be beneficial for China. He argues that the Han and Tang Dynasties both coincided with particularly warm periods in history.[191]

While these scholars are sceptical of some of the scientific conclusions drawn by the IPCC, none expresses substantial disagreement with official government policy on climate change. Perhaps not surprisingly, none of the more outspoken sceptics participated in the 2007 IPCC reports. Sceptical discourses in China make a clear distinction between certain scientific findings, which they may question, and domestic policy statements, which they would not.

Disputing the science of climate change remains the preserve of a small group of academics. There is limited public debate about the integrity of climate science and almost none on natural global warming versus anthropogenic climate change. This is not due to censorship, as climate change is not seen as a sensitive issue, unlike human rights, political freedoms, and other environmental issues such as water pollution. Dissenting voices are relatively free to express their opinions in academic journals or public forums, but it is not a topic that Chinese bloggers or the media have focused on extensively. Instead their attention remains concerned with other issues such as food security and official corruption. Editors do not come under pressure from readers to report more frequently on climate change issues or to advocate a pro-sceptic editorial line.

Both the newspapers chosen for the survey come under the strong influence of the Communist Party and ruling elites. The *People's Daily*

[188] 'Beijing University Professors Doubt IPCC: Global Climate is Not Warming, it is Entering into a Warm Phase', *NetEase*, Beijing, 11 Apr. 2010.
[189] 'Vice-President of CAS Questions IPCC Report: "Emissions Trap" of Developed Countries', China News, Beijing, 16 Apr. 2010: www.chinanews.com.cn/gn/news/2010/04-16/2231837.shtml.
[190] Hongyang Gou, *Low-Carbon Plot* (2010).
[191] The Tang Dynasty (618–907) is often cited as a high point in China's imperial history, with the economy, politics, culture, and military strength reaching unparalleled levels of advancement. This narrative fits with the accusations that the link between human activity and warming is propaganda being pushed by developed countries to constrain the rise of developing countries. However, this discourse has become less credible since scientists found evidence that a shift in monsoons led to drought and famine in the final century of Tang power, leading to its eventual collapse.

is an official party organ, and has the largest circulation of any daily newspaper in China, with 2.3 million in 2008. Official organisations are required to subscribe to it. The general public is thought not to read it and its retail sales are low. The *Beijing Evening News* on the other hand reaches a more 'popular' audience with official daily sales of more than one million copies, making it the most widely circulated of the evening newspapers. It combines hard and soft news in an accessible style.

Academic and other studies suggest that the volume of coverage of climate change increased substantially after the 2007 IPCC reports, often with official encouragement.[192] More than 100 Chinese journalists attended the Copenhagen summit, the largest team from a developing country, and three times more than their number at the 2007 Bali summit. The amount of coverage by the *People's Daily* and the *Beijing Evening News* of the Copenhagen meeting was in the mid-range of the 12 countries monitored, and just behind that of the UK and Italy.[193]

Results

- There were only ten articles quoting sceptics across the two periods, and most of these were generic quotes. The number went up for both newspapers, but as a percentage of its overall coverage of climate change, the figure actually dropped in the case of the *People's Daily*.

- The *Beijing Evening News* had the least number of articles about climate change in all 12 newspapers surveyed.

- Of the ten articles, six were opinion pieces in the *People's Daily*, all of which made some mention of sceptics but to contest their points of view.

- Professor Qian Weihong, from the Department of Atmospheric Sciences at Peking University, was the only named sceptic voice quoted. None of the other Chinese sceptic voices listed above appeared in our sample.

- There was no named foreign sceptic, but there was one reference in the *Beijing Evening News* to the American Enterprise Institute for Public Policy Research, which was described as being 'not only a think tank, but also an advocate of the Bush Administration. It has painstakingly denied that climate warming has something to do with the human emissions of GHGs.'

---

[192] Painter, *Summoned by Science*, 17, and Sandy Tolan, *Coverage of Climate Change in Chinese Media* (2007).
[193] Painter, *Summoned by Science*, 40 and appendices.

Discussion

The very low presence of climate scepticism in our survey was largely due to the two factors: the newspapers' adherence to the official government line on the causes of global warming, and the low volume of coverage of 'Climategate'. As Xin Benjian, an editor at the *People's Daily* expressed it,

> *editorial lines come from the Chinese government. Whilst it is important to report all the issues, including sceptical arguments, if the newspaper gave the impression that scepticism was the main discourse then the editor would be sacked, because this is not the position of the Chinese government.*

Likewise, Cai Wenging, a journalist at the *Beijing Evening News*, explained: 'we have no editorial line on climate change. Editorial comment is provided by the Xinhua News Agency for all international issues, so we follow their opinion. We do not have the relevant documentation to publish our own opinion.'

Editors from both papers said that sceptical voices are only mentioned in parts of long, in-depth articles, and then they would not be featured prominently. As for editorials, as Xin Benjian explained it, 'If mentioned in editorials, the sceptical argument is only given one sentence at most', a view echoed by Cai Wenging who said 'in the interest of providing a story we might mention a sentence or two, but this is just so that a counter-argument can be provided. In this way we acknowledge that sceptics exist.' She also explains that she personally does not include sceptical views as she has had guidance from 'the renowned Chinese scholar Luo Yong that we should not listen to sceptics'.

There were several articles in our sample which did make brief reference to 'Climategate'. Xin Benjian said that it was important to tell their readers the story, 'otherwise they would appear to be prejudiced', whilst the *Beijing Evening News* said it was reported for a few days 'because it was a global issue' and 'because it raised the issue of scientific inaccuracy'. However, as explained by one of the *Beijing Evening News'* editors, Zhang Hui, the whole issue of climate change is not covered much in her paper because her readers are 'not very interested. There are more important issues such as food security.' She adds that 'our readers use online micro-blogging and commenting to let us know their views, but it seems this topic is still one that only minorities and specialists are interested in. There is therefore no great demand for further coverage of this issue, let alone sceptical voices.' This may well go some way to explaining why the paper had the lowest amount of coverage of climate change in both periods we looked at.

It was interesting to note that the *People's Daily* is aware of the views of the leading sceptic Ding Zhongli mentioned above. Xin Benjian explained that in his view it can be

> *difficult to argue that recent human activity affects climate systems that can take tens of thousands of years to form and change. Therefore, some Chinese scientists (like Ding Zhongli) might argue that it is difficult to reach solid conclusions over the extent of human impact based on the IPCC reports, and that more observation is needed. However, in the same breath, Chinese scientists quoted in articles agree that the human impact on the environment is obvious. Regions of China used to be very fertile but now suffer from severe droughts due to the Three Gorges Dam project.*

Finally, of course, Chinese journalists say they are not lobbied by organisations espousing a sceptical viewpoint. As one of them explained, 'The government's power supersedes the power of state enterprises and any other organisations that may wish to lobby.' At a simple but powerful level, this comment represents the main reason why there are so few sceptical voices in the Chinese press: it is not a result of direct censorship, but rather because climate scepticism is not the official line of a government which on most issues exercises huge influence over the Chinese media.

But it is interesting to stress that, contrary to what many outsiders may think, sceptical scientists do exist in China, and sceptical views are discussed relatively openly. For example, an article written in the *People's Daily* in April 2007 by Zheng Guoguang, the general director of the China Meteorological Association and no sceptic, said that there is still 'great scientific uncertainty about climate change'. So there is, as mentioned above, some public questioning of some aspects of climate change, including the speed and severity of its impacts, and the motivations of developed countries. This is climate scepticism with particular Chinese characteristics.

France

by Kheira Belkacem and James Painter

Context

Climate scepticism hardly featured in the French media until an article was published in September 2006 in the widely-read weekly magazine *L'Express* called 'The Snows of Kilimanjaro'. It was authored by Claude

Allègre, a politician, a former Minister of Education (1997–2000) in the Socialist government of Lionel Jospin and a scientist himself (of geochemistry).[194] Since then Allègre has become France's most high-profile sceptic, arguing that clouds and solar activity are more significant factors than CO_2 in causing global warming. He is not above attacking mainstream scientists, at times calling some of them 'religious fanatics', 'Marxists', or 'mediocre scientists'. Allègre is a popular TV interviewee and is particularly influential in the left-leaning press and political class.

France's top scientific body, the Académie des Sciences, held a debate in March 2007 about the causes of global warming, in which mainstream scientists took on the arguments of Allègre and other sceptical scientists who had emerged by this time. Two of the most prominent are Vincent Courtillot and Jean Louis Le Mouël, both geophysicists and both members of the Institut de Physique du Globe de Paris (a research institute of which both Allègre and Courtillot have been directors). Courtillot is a close friend of Allègre and, like him, argues that solar radiation could be the cause of global warming. He also sits on the academic advisory board of the GWPF in London.

Allègre's book 'L'Imposture climatique' (the climate deception), which he published in February 2010, received considerable national coverage and has sold more than 100,000 copies.[195] But it was attacked by hundreds of scientists for being 'full of factual mistakes, distortions of data, and plain lies'. They asked the French science minister, Valérie Pécresse, for another public debate in September 2010. The ensuing report on the debate released in October by the Académie contradicted the claims in Allègre's book.

As mentioned in Chapter 3, a study of 144 articles in *Le Monde* and *Le Figaro* from 2001–7 concluded that the coverage of climate change came mostly in the form of longer news pieces that 'offered due background information' and promoted scientific certainty about climate science.[196] It would seem that, despite Allègre's public profile, in general climate scepticism did not get much coverage. However, some observers say that the combination of 'Climategate', the questioning of the IPCC reports, and the publication of Allègre's book did make a small difference in the period November 2009 to early 2010. 'Climategate' by itself did not get that much coverage as it was usually seen as a British story which hardly affected the basic science. But as Yves Sciama, a science writer for *Science et Vie*, sums up the whole period:

> *My impression is that there was a rise in the coverage of sceptics. Not hundreds of articles, but some. For example, Henri Atlan, a widely-respected biologist, suddenly came out with a sceptic piece in Le Monde. And he wasn't the*

---

[194] Yves Sciama, 'Controverse climatique: Cinq ans de crescendo', *Enquête*, 29 Nov. 2010.
[195] *Le Figaro*, 15 Feb. 2011
[196] Boyce and Lewis (eds), *Climate Change and the Media*, 208–9.

only one. Jean Marc Levy Leblond was another who popped up. Scientists, quite old, quite dominant but not in the niche of climate science, came out with these opinions. They said they were challenging a dictatorship of science.[197]

Some of these opinion pieces appeared in *Le Monde* and *Le Figaro*, which along with *Libération* dominate the French quality print market. *Le Monde* is traditionally known as a moderately left-leaning newspaper, but not as left-wing as *Libération*. *Le Figaro* is a more conservative newspaper, more affiliated to the right wing. There are no real equivalents of the British tabloids. Regional newspapers such as *Ouest-France* enjoy a much higher circulation than the three qualities. Whereas *Le Monde*'s circulation in 2010 was around 320,000 and *Le Figaro* 330,000, *Ouest-France*'s was about 780,000.

The domination of the more elite market by just three well-established newspapers can mean that together they set a *de facto* agenda on coverage of an issue, including that of how much space to give to sceptical viewpoints. It is perhaps significant that two of the papers, *Le Monde* and *Libération*, have two experienced science journalists (Stéphane Foucart and Sylvestre Huet), who remained convinced by the main tenets of mainstream science's explanation of global warming.[198]

Results of survey

- There were a total of only 22 articles quoting sceptics over the two periods in both newspapers, which is both a low number and a low percentage compared to the UK and the USA.

- *Le Monde* actually gave less space to sceptics in 2010 than in 2007 (11% in 2007 and only 5% in 2010), while *Le Figaro* gave slightly more space to sceptics in 2010 than in 2007 (5% of articles in 2007 and 7% in 2010).

- *Le Figaro* focused on French sceptics and hardly mentioned or quoted foreign sceptics. Of the seven the paper quoted, six were French and only one was from the USA (James Inhofe). *Le Monde* quoted a few more foreign sceptics, but only briefly and mainly in its news reporting.

- *Le Monde* only mentioned or quoted sceptics to reject their views, whether in a news report or an opinion piece. *Le Monde* did not give space to sceptics in opinion pieces to express their views. Rather, the three opinion pieces

---

[197] Author interview, July 2011.
[198] See e.g. the blog by Huet, called {sciences}², available at http://sciences.blogs.liberation.fr.

in *Le Monde* which mentioned sceptics were written by scientists who dispute and reject sceptical views.

- *Le Figaro* gave some limited space to sceptics through three opinion pieces where they could express their views and where no dispute or rejection occurred. Two of these opinion pieces were written by a regular columnist, the third by Claude Allègre.[199]

Discussion

Not too much should be read into the fact that *Le Monde*'s inclusion of sceptical voices actually dropped across the two periods of our study. The first period in 2007 coincided with the first debate on the causes of global warming in the Académie des Sciences which may explain the marginally higher mentions. All three of France's most prominent sceptics – Allègre, Courtillot and Le Mouël – were quoted at this time in news reports. *Le Figaro* also quoted the same three in March 2007. What is more interesting to note is that *Le Monde* did not include any sceptical voices in its extensive coverage of the opening of the Copenhagen summit in December 2009, which marks it out from the coverage in many British and American newspapers. It is also interesting to note that, whereas *Le Monde* put an emphasis on the publication of the second part of the fourth IPCC report in 2007, in our search results *Le Figaro* hardly covered the report and rather chose to focus on the European Council meeting in March 2007, where the then French president Jacques Chirac was busy promoting nuclear energy to other EU member states.

The vast majority of the sceptics quoted in most newspapers are French. Apart from the three above, the other one mentioned in our search results is Serge Galam, a physicist, and Research Director of the CNRS (Centre National de la Recherche Scientifique) who strongly opposes IPCC scientists and argues that nothing proves that anthropogenic activities are the main reason for global warming. He is quoted in two opinion pieces in *Le Monde* in February 2007, but is refuted by the mainstream science authors. Stéphane Foucart from *Le Monde* explains the lack of quoting of foreign sceptics by saying that 'I also see and read sceptical publications abroad but I would rather not write a piece on that as there is a strong probability that the findings would be refuted'. Foucart says that his general position is that he quotes 'things that have been published in peer-reviews journals, I quote findings that are generally very difficult to refute'. He has written a piece on four articles written by Le Mouël and Courtillot and published in a minor scientific journal but 'only to refute their findings'.

[199] See *Le Figaro*, 15 Feb. 2010, 1 Dec. 2009, 3 Feb. 2007.

The evidence from our survey would suggest that 'Climategate' did not have much impact on the little – if any – amount of uncontested space *Le Monde* generally gives to sceptical voices. However, in the case of *Le Figaro*, it may have had an impact on the paper's willingness to offer a platform in the opinion columns. As mentioned above, Claude Allègre and a columnist, Yves de Kerdrel, were given opinion pieces in December 2009 and February 2010. Foucart says that in *Le Monde*, as in US newspapers, the distinction between articles by science journalists and opinion pieces is important, and that in his view sceptics have only been given credibility in the opinion pages of the paper. These may have fallen outside the period of our study.[200] But Foucart adds that 'we make sure in *Le Monde* that we do not include any sort of confusion when it comes to scientific facts'. It is difficult to get an accurate picture of the effect on journalists of 'Climategate' on *Le Figaro* as no one there was able to give an interview, but some observers like Yves Sciama say there have been important divisions within the science writing team there with some of the journalists much more sympathetic to sceptic positions than others.[201]

However, it is interesting to note that in a survey of *Le Figaro* readers in February 2010, 70% of respondents said they did have doubts about the causes of global warming, and 30% said they didn't. Foucart says that some pressure does come from the readers of *Le Monde* to include more sceptical viewpoints, such as those of Courtillot. He says the internet plays a major role in this as letters from readers show they have read sceptical blogs. He also thinks small right-wing French think tanks such as the Institut Hayek and Institut Turgot do have an influence, as they publish information online accusing journalists at *Le Monde*, *Le Figaro*, and *Libération* of being biased, which can have an impact on editors. He says the paper has received strongly virulent and anonymous criticism which is 'almost libellous', and this has increased since 2009.

In conclusion, the two French newspapers do stand out from those in the UK and the USA for giving little space to sceptics, despite the presence of the high-profile telegenic sceptic, Claude Allègre. It is of interest that Allègre belongs to a socialist party, which may make him one of the few examples in the world of a prominent left-wing sceptic. But he is widely regarded on the left as being something of a maverick.

In general though, sceptical views are only found on the fringes of the main political parties. Not even the National Front's official position questions the basics of climate science, which marks it out from the British National Party and UKIP. Another key difference is that around 80% of the French electricity production comes from nuclear plants, and the nuclear industry (which would of course benefit from a general

---

[200] See e.g. the article by Henri Atlan, *Le Monde*, 28 Mar. 2010, which came after our second period of study, and the blog by Sylvestre Huet at http://sciences.blogs.liberation.fr/home/2010/04/mod%C3%A8le-climatique-une-r%C3%A9ponse-%C3%A0-henri-atlan-et-levyleblond.html.
[201] Marc Menessier who works at *Le Figaro* is a friend of Allègre and has written a book with him, whereas Caroline de Malet, another journalist on the paper, has posted comments on her blog against the sceptics.

move away from fossil fuels) has strong links with both the right-wing and the Socialist Party. Heavy state investment in the nuclear industry and in other key sectors of the economy goes back to President de Gaulle and was a strategic industrial choice by the whole political class. This also leaves little political space for anything comparable to some of the lobby groups in the UK or the ones in the USA with funding from fossil fuel industries.

There is a wider point, as Yves Sciama explains it:

> France has a rationalist, engineer culture and people who have gone to engineer schools often end up in politics or influential positions. This entire social class of powerful engineers has links with the nuclear lobby. I would also say there is a tradition of respecting the science and not challenging the experts which is quite strong in France. This is probably why climate change was accepted very early.

This respect for the science may also partly explain why experienced science journalists with strong views on the primacy of the science are more likely to wield considerable sway over the overall editorial direction of a newspaper. A final distinguishing feature is the absence in France of a tabloid culture with a strong political or quasi-campaigning agenda. There are no equivalents of the British *Daily Mail* or *Daily Express*.

India

by Anu Jogesh and James Painter

Context

Both the *Times of India* (*TOI*) and *The Hindu* are English-language broadsheet dailies with a pan-India circulation. The *TOI* has the widest circulation of all English-language newspapers globally, and an estimated readership in 2010 of just over 7m readers. *The Hindu* – with a strong base in the southern state of Tamil Nadu where it is headquartered – has more than 2m readers, which makes it the third highest in India among English dailies, after the *TOI* and *Hindustan Times*.

India does not have a pan-India culture of tabloid news consumption. Rather, vernacular news channels have taken the place of the newspaper tabloid in terms of both their content and their viewership profile. English-language newspapers such as the *TOI* and *The Hindu* cater to a smaller English-speaking section of the country compared to Indian-language newspapers, which garner a much larger readership. But English-language newspapers offer more column space to climate-

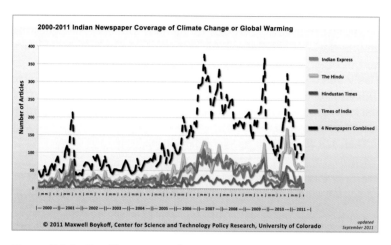

Figure 5.1. Indian Newspaper Coverage of Climate Change or Global Warming, 2000–11

related news. Both newspapers currently have dedicated environment reporters.

Previous academic research (which is not extensive) on the coverage of climate change in the Indian media suggests three trends: (a) a growing amount of coverage in the English-language press since 2007; (b) a dominant framing of the issue as reflecting the world's North–South divide; and (c) a virtual absence of climate scepticism.

As regards the first point, Figure 5.1 shows the general increase over the period 2000–11, but with high peaks and troughs after early 2007. Two studies of the UN's Copenhagen talks in December 2009 showed the extensive coverage by the Indian media in general and by the *TOI* in particular of the summit. [202] The *TOI* generated 52 climate-related articles over a six-day period at the start and end of the summit. This was the second highest amount of the 24 newspapers from 12 countries that were examined (less than *Folha de São Paulo* but more than the *Guardian* in the UK). *The Hindu* did not really pay attention to climate change until the Copenhagen summit.

As regards the second point, an extensive study of climate news coverage in four Indian national dailies between 2002 and 2007 by the UK academic Simon Billet concluded the Indian media was predominantly nationalistic in its treatment, placing the onus for action on industrialised nations.[203] A forthcoming study by Max Boykoff and Emily Boyd of a later period (2004–9) also stresses that the 'villain-victim' discourse, where India is the victim and the West is the villain, is very common.[204] A 2011 study for the Centre for Policy Research (CPR) found that the debate in the Indian print media had widened since the Billet report especially in the run-up to the Copenhagen

---

[202] Painter, *Summoned by Science*, 40, and Boykoff, 'Indian Media Representations'.
[203] Billet, 'Dividing Climate Change'.
[204] Boykoff lecture, Oxford, July 2011.

conference, and that the nationalistic narrative, to some extent, was being counteracted by reports and opinion pieces that favoured India taking on unsupported action.[205]

As Professor Lavanya Rajami of the CPR in New Delhi expresses it, there have been two dominant narratives in the Indian media coverage of climate change, the first being the 'development needs of India versus environmental concerns of the world' and the other being the 'equity debate' over who – the West or the Rest – should pay the greater price for cutting GHG emissions.[206] The dominance of these two narratives leaves scant room for climate scepticism. The Billet study concludes that there is very little scepticism in the Indian press, with 98% of the articles directly attributing climate change to anthropogenic causes. The 2011 CPR study found that in the three months prior to and after Copenhagen across nine Indian newspapers, only 2% of the articles carried sceptical voices.

There is very little organised scepticism in India. The right-wing Liberty Institute in Delhi did start to question aspects of the science of climate change publicly in mid-2009 in the run-up to the Copenhagen summit, and representatives appeared on a few occasions on an English-language news channel. This was partly in response to the questioning of the data for the melting of the Himalayas and of the chair of the IPCC, Rajendra Pachauri, which for obvious reasons received considerably more play than 'Climategate' in India. In this sense, a different choice of period for our study might have yielded slightly different results. There are no political parties or business groups that have made any concerted effort to oppose climate science, but there are some individual scientists such as geophysicist Jarandhan Negi, and the former chairman of the India Space Research Organisation, UR Rao, and Dr RK Ganjoo, director of the Institute of Himalayan Glaciology in Jammu University, who through their research have attributed global warming to other factors such as solar activity. There are other individuals quoted in the press who are sceptical in different ways.[207]

Part of the reason why these voices have not been heard much is the high profile of prominent individuals like Dr Pachauri and non-governmental organisations (such as the Center for Science and Environment, Greenpeace India, WWF India, or The Energy Research Institute). They have been vocal about the risks and impacts of man-made climate change and seem to have wielded a significant influence on climate reporting. They often enjoy close relationships with Indian environment reporters.

---

[205] A. Jogesh, 'A Change in Climate? Examining Trends in Climate Change Reportage in the Indian Print Media', in Navroz K. Dubash (ed.), *Handbook on Climate Change and India* (forthcoming).

[206] Author interview, Oxford, June 2011.

[207] The *TOI*'s associate editor Jug Suriya; *The Economic Times* consulting editor Swaminathan Ankelesaria Aiyar; R Gopalakrishnan, Director of Tata Sons, one of India's well-known business houses; the member of opposition party Sitaram Yechury; and theoretical geophysicist Janardan Negi have all voiced varying degrees of uncertainty about climate change in the Indian press.

Results

- As row 2 of Table 4.1 shows, the number of articles with sceptical voices in the Indian press is low, but it did increase for both newspapers over the two periods. The increase was most marked for *The Hindu*. However, row 3 shows that in percentage terms, the number actually dropped for the *TOI*.

- The *TOI* has been relatively more consistent in terms of the frequency of its climate reporting as well as the portrayal of sceptical voices (between 2007 and 2009/10) as compared to *The Hindu* whose output on this topic was very low in 2007. *The Hindu* had a slightly higher percentage of sceptical voices in 2009/10 despite the fact that its absolute number of climate articles still trailed behind the *TOI* in that period.

- Many of the articles in both newspapers quoted sceptics generically. For example, in the second period, half of the articles in *The Hindu* (9 out of 18) refer to sceptics in a generic fashion (and an almost similar number, 8 out of 18, in fact defend climate science even as they quote or refer to sceptics). In the same period, three out of the seven pieces in the *TOI* refer to sceptics generically.

- What is perhaps most noteworthy is that between 50% and 70% of the articles with sceptical voices (except in *The Hindu* in the first period) are internationally sourced (i.e. either from international wires or publications like the *Guardian* or *NYT*).

- India clearly has a handful of its own sceptical columnists such as Swaminathan Ankelaseria Aiyar of the *TOI* and MJ Akbar, former editor of the *Asian Age* (who has an opinion piece in the *TOI* in the period selected). Despite the fact that the majority of the reports in the *TOI* have a clear tilt towards an acceptance of climate science, these opinion pieces are also given occasional column space. However, neither of the two – Aiyar or Akbar – is an outright climate denier.

- Of the seven sceptical voices quoted in *The Hindu* over the two periods, all seven were international, while for the *TOI* over the same period 16 out of the 19 were international.

Discussion

Most of the opinion pieces mentioning sceptics that appeared in the *TOI* were related to 'Climategate' and 'Himalayagate'. Jug Suriya, the author of one of them, is not a scientist by background but rather a columnist who usually presents a (sometimes comic) counterview to whatever is the dominant thinking on an issue. He tends not to question the science but more the policy options. Swaminathan Ankelaseria Aiyar is an economist who also examines the possible costs of adjustment measures. As in many newspapers around the world, the *TOI* does not have a single unified editorial policy on climate change, and gives air to sceptic views within its column pages.

The small number of opinion pieces need to be seen in the overall context of the Indian media's reaction to the two controversies. The 2011 CPR study found that 122 newspaper articles were written about 'Climategate' and 'Himalayagate' between September 2009 and March 2010. Of these 43% directly defended or quoted individuals who defended the IPCC and by extension the veracity of anthropogenic climate research done by the body of scientists under it. The others did not always question the veracity of the science behind climate change, but rather argued that the IPCC process was flawed.

Priscilla Jebaraj, one of the regular environment reporters on *The Hindu*, says that 'Climategate' made no difference to whether she quotes sceptics or not, as the paper has never run a story of hers which quotes them. She has considered running stories with sceptics in them (such as a sceptical report by the Heritage Foundation) and has interviewed Lord Monckton, but either the editor has said he did not think it was worth doing (in the case of the Heritage Foundation) or there was not enough space in the paper (in the case of Lord Monckton). As she points out, even in the case of 'Himalayagate', the basic science of climate change was not questioned, rather the pace of the impacts. Priscilla Jebaraj also says *The Hindu* carries international articles from left-leaning publications like the *Guardian* or the *NYT*, so perhaps 'a sceptical figure who is a Republican will not find space on the paper'. It is perhaps of significance then that it is the more liberal *TOI* that has given more space to (Indian) sceptical columnists than the left-leaning *The Hindu*.

Nitin Sethi, who is a special correspondent on the *TOI* who regularly writes about climate change issues, says he has a broadly free hand from his editors on what stories and what angles to cover, including whether to include sceptical voices. He says he did write a lot about 'Himalayagate' in part because it turned into a dispute between the Indian government and the (Indian) head of the IPCC. He does not remember ever having written a story which outright rejected the consensus on climate science. He says he has found about 8–10 articles in scientific journals carrying sceptical voices, but he has been 'sceptical about picking them up. My first question has been to ask if I can find their sources of funding or affiliation.' Finally, Nitin Sethi says he is not aware of any coordinated lobbying attempts by sceptics in India. On the contrary, he says the voice of the climate change 'believers' is so strong that he is wary of civil society and the 500 local and internationally affiliated NGOs he says there are in India which are pushing the government to do more on climate change. 'The pro-climate, climate-getting-worse voices are far more high-pitched here than the sceptics are', he says.

Indian environment journalists will often point out that the 'local weather impacts' narrative of the story – changes in the timing of monsoons, more droughts, and the like – is a major shaper of their reporting and a countervailing force to any sceptical voices. However, they do say that there are more 'sceptical' voices emerging about India's policies towards tackling climate change or the (lack of) progress at the international negotiations and India's role within them.

In summary then, various factors help to explain the scant presence of sceptical voices in the Indian media: the absence of business-linked lobby groups, the presence of strong civil society organisations convinced by the science of climate change and the need to act, the dominant framing of the issue in the media as a nationalistic 'us-versus-them' narrative, the paucity of climate-sceptical scientists in India or throughout South Asia, and a journalistic culture (at least in the two newspapers we examined) which pays little attention to those questioning the basic science of climate change.

USA

Context

The discussion in Chapter 2 of the nature of American 'exceptionalism', and in particular the political polarisation of discussions about climate change, forms the essential context for understanding the difference between the coverage in the *New York Times* and the *Wall Street Journal*. The two newspapers are widely regarded as 'trend-setting news outlets of record' in the United States, their coverage 'strongly shapes the editorial decisions made by broadcast and cable networks', and they are often targeted by 'advocates on both sides of the debate'.[208] Even though we used the print version and not the online version of the newspapers for the content analysis, virtually all the articles on the print version end up on the websites, which are two of the most heavily visited news sites in the USA and abroad. For example, according to the Pew Project for Excellence in Journalism, the website of the *WSJ* is the top source for public affairs information for business leaders and professionals.[209]

---

[208] Nisbet, *Climate Shift*, 67.
[209] Pew Project for Excellence in Journalism, *2010 State of the Media Report*, quoted in *Climate Shift*, 67.

The *New York Times* had a circulation of about 875,000 in 2010 (the third largest in the USA) and 34m unique web visitors from the USA in May 2011. It is well-known for its liberal slant and targets an audience from upper socio-economic groups. Historically it has enjoyed a dedicated and specialist team of science and environment reporters. In 2009, it created an environment desk separate to its science desk. 2009 was also the year that its former environment correspondent, Andy Revkin, who is widely regarded as one of the most experienced reporters on climate change, left to write his own influential blog called Dot Earth.

Since 2007 the *Wall Street Journal* has been owned by Rupert Murdoch's News Corporation, which also owns Fox News and the *New York Post*. In April 2011 the paper enjoyed the largest circulation of any US newspaper at around 2.1m. Prior to April, its circulation revenue had grown 17 straight quarters in a row, while its digital subscriptions had increased as well, by nearly 22% in a year to over half a million.[210] It targets a similar audience profile to the *NYT*. Historically, it has been known for a division between its liberal or 'straight' news reporting and the more conservative, free-market leanings of its editorial and opinion pages. Max Boykoff's 2007 paper, 'Flogging a Dead Norm?', for example, found that the *WSJ* fitted the general pattern of 'balanced' reporting no longer being evident in the five papers he looked at.[211] Its opinion pages however are widely seen as different. For example, it has a long history of offering space there to different types of well-known climate sceptics like Richard Lindzen, Fred Singer, and Bjørn Lomborg, all whom were mentioned in Chapter 2.

A wider picture of media outlets belonging to News Corporation pushing an essentially sceptical point of view in its opinion articles is advanced by the Australian media scholar, David McKnight. In his study of the newspaper *The Australian,* Fox News, and the *Sun* and *Times/Sunday Times* in the UK during the period 1997 to 2007 (which obviously did not include the *Wall Street Journal*), McKnight found that 'newspapers and television stations owned by News Corporation, based on their editorials, columnists and commentators, largely denied the science of climate change and dismissed those who were concerned about it'.[212] However, the McKnight study also found that commentary on climate change was at its most sceptical in Australia and the USA compared to that found in the UK newspapers. This is a theme we shall return to in our discussion of the UK findings in the next chapter, where we will argue that the influence of James Murdoch has probably been a major factor.

McKnight found that climate science was often characterised as a form of 'political correctness', a term which became widely known as a derogatory label for the right. This would certainly seem to be a framing

---

[210] Its success prompted former *Guardian* editor Peter Preston to comment that 'You don't need to love Rupert Murdoch to admire what he's done with the WSJ'. See Peter Preston, 'Hold the Front Page – it's Time US Papers Had a Redesign', *Observer*, 8 May 2011.
[211] Boykoff, 'Flogging a Dead Norm'.
[212] David McKnight, 'A Change in the Climate?', *Journalism*, 11/6 (2010), 693.

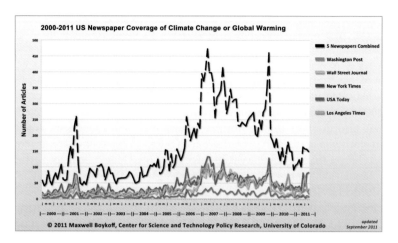

2000-2011 US Newspaper Coverage of Climate Change or Global Warming

© 2011 Maxwell Boykoff, Center for Science and Technology Policy Research, University of Colorado

Figure 5.2 US Newspaper Coverage of Climate Change or Global Warming, 2000–2011

of the issue that commentators at Fox News are happy to promote. A less political but essentially sceptical framing of climate science was revealed by a memo sent by Washington managing editor Bill Sammon to Fox News anchors and reporters in the run-up to the Copenhagen summit in December 2009. The memo asked them to

> *refrain from asserting that the planet has warmed (or cooled) in any given period without IMMEDIATELY pointing out that such theories are based upon data that critics have called into question. It is not our place as journalists to assert such notions as facts, especially as this debate intensifies.*[213]

Historically, since 2000 both the *WSJ* and the *NYT* have gone through peaks and troughs in the amount of coverage they have given to global warming and climate change. The strongest peaks have been in 2007 and from late 2009 to early 2010.

The raw numbers on which Figure 5.2 is based show that the *WSJ* averaged about 80 articles for the period February to April 2007, and the *NYT* about 115, while for the period of November 2009 to February 2010 the totals were about 60 and 80 respectively. In April 2007, both papers registered their highest number of articles in one month for the whole of the period 2000–11. In February and March 2007, and from December 2009 to February 2010, the *NYT* had the largest number of articles of the five papers dedicated to climate change and global warming.[214]

---

[213] Quoted in Fong and Jencks, 'Report Glosses Over Media Failures in Climate Coverage'.
[214] Based on Max Boykoff and Maria Mansfield's summary of data from 2000–11.

Main findings

In both newspapers the number of articles and the percentage of articles with sceptical voices within them went up, from 21% to 29% in the case of the *NYT*, and from 13% to 40% in the case of the *WSJ*. Clearly the percentage increase was much higher in the *WSJ*. (See row 3 of Table 4.1.)

There are other clear distinctions between the two newspapers:

- As we saw in Chapter 4, over the two periods the percentage of opinion pieces and editorials quoting sceptical voices was significantly higher in the case of the *WSJ*: 64% compared to 43% in the *NYT*. In other words, sceptical voices were more likely to be heard in the opinion pieces and editorials in the *WSJ* than in its news reporting, whereas for the *NYT* it is the reverse.

- The number of articles on the news pages quoting individual sceptical voices in the *NYT* hardly increased over the two periods (from 10 to 11), despite the 'Climategate' affair. In contrast, the equivalent figure for the *WSJ* went up from 2 to 7. In the *NYT*, nearly half the articles on the news pages quoting sceptics in the second period were examples of generic quoting, perhaps reflecting the way it reported 'Climategate'.

- The biggest difference is to be found in the opinion pieces and editorials. In the former category, all 14 articles across the two periods in the *NYT* were those where the author included sceptical voices essentially to dispute them or reject them. In contrast, of the 17 opinion pieces found in the *WSJ*, only one fitted this category. (See Table 4.2 in Chapter 4.) In other words, the *WSJ* gave plenty of space to sceptical voices without their being challenged. Amongst their invited columnists were well-known sceptical voices such as Bjørn Lomborg (five times), Philip Stott, Richard Lindzen, and Nigel Lawson (once each).

- As regards editorials, the *NYT* published 10 mentioning sceptical voices, but all 10 fitted the category 'where their views are disputed or rejected, or where the conclusions are measured'. In sharp contrast, only one of the 12 *WSJ* editorials mentioning sceptical voices fitted this category. The remaining 11 fell into the first two categories of (i) where the consensus on climate change science is seriously questioned, or (ii) where the tone is in general sceptical of measures to combat climate change.

• In the *NYT* the number of sceptics quoted in all types of articles actually decreased from 23 to 19 over the two periods, whereas in the *WSJ* the number went up considerably from 5 to 18.

Discussion

These results should not perhaps come as a surprise to anyone familiar with the two newspapers. In its editorials, the *NYT* has consistently followed a line that global warming is happening, is largely man-made, and urgent government action is needed to combat it. In contrast, the *WSJ* has consistently maintained that carbon emissions may play a role in global warming, but that the case is not sufficiently proven to justify a massive change in energy use. Typical is its editorial of 5 February 2007 which played down the importance of the first IPCC report of that year.[215] In it, the paper states that its readers should 'beware claims that the science of global warming is settled' and goes on to praise the work of the British sceptic Lord Monckton for his 'voice of sanity on global warming'. The *NYT*'s editorial on the same day could hardly be more at variance.[216] It starts off with the words 'Should Congress require any further reason to move aggressively to limit greenhouse gas emissions, it need only read Friday's report from the Intergovernmental Panel on Climate Change, the world's authoritative voice on global warming.'

The difference between the two newspapers falls broadly in line with the findings of other studies based on content analysis of the US media. As discussed previously, our study used a different methodology to the one used in the 2011 report *Climate Shift*. But at least in the case of opinion articles and editorials, our results would seem to support its findings that the *WSJ* is far more likely than the *NYT* to publish pieces which are in some way sceptical. We found that of the 24 articles on the opinion and editorial pages on the *NYT* quoting sceptics, there were none where those voices were uncontested. In contrast, at the *WSJ*, of the 29 articles, 27 were uncontested.

The *Climate Shift* report concludes that in the *NYT* over the period 2009/10, approximately nine of ten news and opinion articles reflected the 'consensus view' on climate change (namely that 'climate change is real and human-caused'). There was a decline between the pre-Copenhagen period, where the 'consensus view' was found in 98% of all articles, to the post-Copenhagen period, where the figure was 87%, but in general the *NYT* was broadly in line with three of the four other newspapers or websites included in the study (*Washington Post*, CNN. com, and Politico).[217]

---

[215] 'Climate of Opinion', editorial, *Wall Street Journal*, 5 Feb. 2007.
[216] 'At Humanity's Doorstep', editorial, *New York Times*, 5 Feb. 2007.
[217] The 'falsely balanced view' was slightly more prevalent in the opinion articles than in the news articles (17% compared to 13%) in the post-Copenhagen period.

In sharp contrast were the results from the *WSJ*. The same study found that the 'consensus view' fell from 76% of all news and opinion articles in the pre-Copenhagen period to 55% in the second period.[218] It was particularly noticeable in the opinion articles where it slipped from 50% to 30%, compared to the news articles where the fall was less pronounced (92% to 79%). Across the two-year period, 'at least eight of 10 news articles at the paper reflected the consensus view, but at the opinion pages, less than half of the articles asserted that climate change was real and that humans were a cause'.[219] A similar result was reached by Scott A. Mandia, a professor of Physical Sciences at Suffolk County Community College, Long Island.[220] He analysed 86 editorials and op-ed pieces in the *WSJ* between October 2008 and late January 2011, and concluded that 7% of them supported the scientific consensus, whereas the rest either did not support the consensus, or ignored all mention of the causes or were focused on non-science issues such as a carbon tax. Professor Mandia commented that the *WSJ*'s percentage breakdown was the 'opposite of the scientific consensus'.

It is also interesting to note that, according to *Climate Shift*, of the five news outlets, the *WSJ* continued to pay considerably more attention to 'Climategate' after December 2009 than the other four. In December, articles in the paper represented about a quarter of all the articles in the five outlets mentioning the affair. From January to August 2010, more than half of all the articles referencing the link to 'Climategate' appeared in the *WSJ*. Curtis Brainard of the Columbia Journalism Review says that 'the Journal already had a fiscally and socially conservative editorial board, and when climate change became a big story, it was only to be expected that the paper would resist the science and most policies to address climate change'.[221] And he adds that when 'Climategate' happened, 'it did make a big splash in terms of emboldening people, including the Journal editorial board and conservative politicians'. Brainard says that, in contrast, the news reporting of climate change-related issues on the *WSJ* remained free of ideology, with what he describes as high-quality in-depth reporting of environment and energy policy issues.

Andy Revkin of the *NYT* says that 'Climategate' did not fundamentally change the way he reported climate science. He says he approached the issue with the same journalistic scepticism all the way through, and tried not only to report what people say but to get behind the motivations and backgrounds of the people involved, as there are so many different types of climate scepticism. He says that there were newspapers or other media

[218] The decline in the percentage of articles reflecting scientific consensus was most marked in the WSJ of any of the five news outlets studied. The figures are 21% for the WSJ, 13% for Politico, 11% for NYT, and 5% for the *Washington Post*. Only CNN registered no decline. Some commentators argue that 'Climategate' shifted the way all the US media presented the science, even though the leaked emails were not found to have undermined the essential science supporting man-made global warming. See Fong and Jencks, 'Report Glosses Over Media Failures in Climate Coverage'.
[219] Nisbet, *Climate Shift*, 71.
[220] Guest blog by Professor Mandia, 'Wall Street Journal; Selectively Pro-Science', *Climate Progress*, 31 Jan. 2011.
[221] Author interview, July 2011. We were unable to get the views of journalists working at the *WSJ*.

that 'perhaps blindly rode the consensus science from the IPCC and other organisations, and felt a sense of potential betrayal. Afterwards it required them to be more circumspect, and this was much more evident in England than in the USA.'[222] Revkin also says that the editorial board of the *NYT* did not 'move one inch' after 'Climategate' in its attitude as reflected in its editorials on a range of issues related to climate change. Nor can he remember ever being told 'we need a sceptical voice in this story'.

In conclusion then, there does seem overwhelming evidence that what mainly drives the difference between the portrayal of climate change – on the opinion pages – in the two newspapers is one of political perspective. The presence on the *WSJ*'s opinion pages of plenty of sceptical voices chimes with its free-market, pro-business leanings which would oppose any strong state intervention to deal with climate change. As for the *NYT*, Curtis Brainard says it is not a matter of the paper being liberal or left-leaning:

> *It's not simple ideology; it's more that the Times is not blinded by ideology. They do not oversell a particular way to addressing the problem either. They're not perfect, but they have been quite careful, for example, in the recent coverage of the possible links between extreme weather and climate change. They are really attentive to the science with a good team of science reporters.*

[222] Author interview, July 2011.

6. Climate Scepticism in the UK Print Media

As we mentioned in Chapter 2, all the main political parties in the UK agree with the mainstream science of climate change. Only UKIP and the BNP are officially sceptical. The leader of the Conservative Party, David Cameron, saw the environment as a key way of recentring the party and from 2006 was outspoken on a number of green issues including global warming. Famously, he travelled to Svalbard in the Arctic in 2006 to highlight his concern. However, there have always been voices on the edges of the party, and within right-wing newspapers who agree with them, who have been opposed to his giving priority to such an issue or to spending considerable sums of money in combating it. They include such names as David Davis, John Redwood, Lord Lawson, and several Conservative MEPs, all of whom, as can be seen in Appendix 4, were quoted fairly extensively in the periods we examined. Many of the top Conservative bloggers are also climate sceptics. So the political context for the UK media's treatment is distinct to that of the USA, for example, as there is much less of a clear right–left split.

We expanded the study of the UK print media from two to ten national newspapers, mainly to test further the extent of the possible correspondence between the dominant political perspective of a paper and the prevalence of climate-sceptical voices: the *Express* and *Sunday Express*, the *Financial Times*, the *Guardian* and its stablemates the *Observer*, the *Independent* and *Independent on Sunday*, the *Mail* and *Mail on Sunday*, the *Mirror* and *Sunday Mirror*, the *Star* and its Sunday edition, the *Sun*, the *Telegraph* and *Sunday Telegraph*, and *The Times* and *Sunday Times*.[223]

The UK print media landscape is interesting for several reasons relevant to our study: it has ten national newspapers all competing for readership, a high degree of polarised political divergence, and a strong 'tabloid' culture. Five of the ten are regarded as 'quality' or 'prestige' newspapers (*The Times, Daily Telegraph, Financial Times, Guardian, Independent*, and their Sunday stable mates), two are mid-market 'black-top' tabloids (the *Mail* and *Express*), and three are downmarket 'red-top' tabloids (the *Sun*, the *Mirror*,

---

[223] We could not include what was until July 2011 the *Sun*'s sister newspaper, the *News of the World*, because it was not available on the Lexis-Nexis or Factiva search engines. The *Financial Times* has a weekend edition, which was included.

and the *Star*). All ten have been included in our study. Regional newspapers in the UK tend not to be strong, unlike in the USA, Australia, and France.

The five 'qualities' tend to aim at a well-educated, affluent, and influential readership, usually considered to be from the AB1 socio-economic groups. Within them, *The Times* and *Telegraph* are usually associated with 'right-of-centre politics that generally support establishment, industry and conservative positions'.[224] The *FT* is generally pro-market, and broadly centre-right. The *Guardian* is more left-of-centre, while the *Independent* prides itself on being independent (though is often liberal or left-of-centre on many issues). The *Mail* and *Express* are both right-wing, and have an audience described loosely as 'middle England', 'moderately affluent and often socially and morally conservative'.[225] The *Sun* and *Star* are generally more right-leaning and the *Mirror* more left-leaning. They all tend to aim at lower income groups. Defining features of tabloids are that they devote

> *relatively little attention to politics, economics and society and relatively much to diversions like sports, scandal and popular entertainment; [and] relatively much attention to the personal and private lives of people, both celebrities and ordinary people, and relatively little to political processes, economic developments and social changes.*[226]

The Times, Sunday Times, News of the World (before its closure in July 2011 due to the hacking scandal), and the *Sun* are owned by Rupert Murdoch's News International. James Murdoch took over responsibility for these papers in 2007. The *Guardian* is owned by the Scott Trust, whilst the *Independent* was bought by Russian billionaire Alexander Lebedev in 2010. Richard Desmond owns the *Express* and the *Star*, and has withdrawn his papers from the system of press self-regulation overseen by the Press Complaints Commission. The *Mail* is published by the Daily Mail and General Trust company whose main shareholder is Viscount Rothermere. It has been run for the last 20 years by its powerful editor Paul Dacre, and the paper remains hugely influential with the political classes. The *Mirror* is owned by the Trinity Mirror Group, while the *Telegraph*s have been owned since 2004 by the Barclay brothers. Tony Gallagher came to the *Daily Telegraph* in 2006 with several other journalists from the *Mail*, and became editor in 2009. It is important to stress that in some cases, and particularly that of the

[224] Alex Lockwood, 'Preparations for a Post-Kyoto Media Coverage of UK Climate Policy', in Boyce and Lewis (eds), *Climate Change and the Media*, 188. For more details of the different newspaper's political leanings, see also Anabela Carvalho, 'Ideological Cultures and Media Discourses on Scientific Knowledge: Re-Reading News on Climate Change', *Public Understanding of Science*, 16 (2007), 223–43; Boykoff and Mansfield, 'Ye Olde Hot Aire'; and Hugh Doulton and Katrina Brown, 'Ten Years to Prevent Catastrophe?', *Global Environment Change*, 19 (2009), 191–202.

[225] Brian McNair, *Journalism and Democracy* (London: Routledge, 2000), 16, quoted in Lockwood (n. 224).

[226] Colin Sparks and John Tulloch (eds), *Tabloid Tales: Global Debates over Media Standards* (Lanham, MD, and Oxford: Rowman & Littlefield, 2000), 10. Tabloids have also been described as being 'more steeped in opinions and commentary as well as personalised writing', and having 'less breadth and depth', and 'more simplistic and sensationalist' representations – see Boykoff and Mansfield, 'Ye Olde Hot Aire', 2.

Telegraph, the Sunday edition of a newspaper can have a different set of editorial priorities and focus to that of its daily counterpart. (See discussion in Appendix 3.)

Table 6.1 shows the wide differences between the circulations of the ten newspapers in December 2010. All ten newspapers and their Sunday counterparts suffered declines over the previous year, although this varied between just 3% for the *Financial Times* and 4% for the *Daily Mail*, to 14% for *The Times* and 12% for the *Guardian*. Even though the *Express*'s circulation is declining, it is still easily larger than the *Guardian* and *Independent* combined. The *Mail*'s circulation has held up well, while its online site had climbed by mid-2011 to be the second most read 'news' website in English after the *New York Times* with 80m unique visitors. The figures in the table are for circulation (including bulks), not readership. The *Sun* for example has an estimated 7.7m readers on a circulation of 2.7m.

Table 6.1. Daily and Sunday Circulation of UK National Newspapers, 2009–10

	Dec. 2010	Dec. 2009	% change
Sun	2,717,013	2,862,935	-5.1
Daily Mirror	1,133,440	1,225,502	-7.51
Daily Star	713,602	784,958	-9.09
Daily Mail	2,030,968	2,113,134	-3.89
Daily Express	623,689	677,750	-7.98
Daily Telegraph	631,280	703,249	-10.23
The Times	448,463	521,535	-14.01
Financial Times	390,121	400,827	-2.67
Guardian	264,819	300,540	-11.89
Independent	175,002	186,940	-6.39
News of the World	2,600,985	2,791,773	-6.83
Sunday Mirror	1,047,363	1,113,310	-5.92
Sunday Mail	352,300	386,920	-8.95
Daily Star Sunday	336,868	353,249	-4.64
Mail on Sunday	1,951,783	2,000,473	-2.43
Sunday Express	544,870	590,596	-7.74
Sunday Times	1,008,163	1,113,195	-9.44
Sunday Telegraph	490,322	525,088	-6.62
Observer	301,457	351,019	-14.12
Independent on Sunday	150,437	155,460	-3.23

Even though the majority of readers of the *Sun* and the *Mirror* come from lower socio-economic groups, it is worth remembering that there are six times more ABC1 readers of the *Sun* (2.8m in May 2011) than there are of the *Independent*, three times more than the *Guardian,* and more than twice that of *The Times*.[227] Likewise, the *News of the World* had an ABC1 readership of 2.9m – more than the *Sunday Times* and

[227] Peter Preston, 'Shock, Horror: The Top People's Paper is the Soaraway Sun', *Observer*, 12 June 2011.

more than the *Sunday Telegraph, Observer,* and *Independent on Sunday* put together. The *Mail* and the *Express* are the only dailies with more women readers than men. As for the age profile of readers, the *Sun* has 4.3m readers aged 15 to 44, compared to 570,000 for the *Guardian* and 410,000 for the *Telegraph*.

Climate change coverage

The *Sun*'s readership profile is one of the factors shaping its generally mainstream reporting of climate change, according to the paper's environment editor, Ben Jackson. He says its readership is younger than that of the *Express* or *Mail* for example, and probably this part of the *Sun*'s readership is more open-minded about the science around man-made global warming. He also says that James Murdoch, who is widely known to be concerned about global warming and has a background in environment sciences, influenced the move to ensure more in-depth reporting of the issue and the environment in general by overseeing the appointment of environment editors on the *Sun* (and *The Times*).[228] Until recently, the *Sun* had two prominent sceptical columnists, Kelvin MacKenzie and Jeremy Clarkson, about whom James Murdoch has commented 'I don't tell people what to write'.[229] Like the *Sun,* the *Mirror* has a dedicated environment (and science) editor, but does not employ sceptical opinion writers. The *Star* stands out from all ten newspapers for its scant coverage of the topic.

Another member of the Murdoch stable, *The Times*, has the same reputation as the *Sun* for generally reflecting the mainstream consensus on climate science in its reporting. It does occasionally give opinion columns to sceptics (like Nigel and Dominic Lawson), but in general it has far fewer sceptical columns than the *Telegraph*, for example. In early 2010 the *Sunday Times* carried a number of news articles highlighting the real and alleged errors in the IPCC reports, but was forced to issue a correction over its reporting of supposed errors by the IPCC on the potential impacts of climate change on the Amazon.[230]

The opinion pages of the *Telegraph* group have at the same time both strongly sceptic voices, such as Christopher Booker on the Sunday edition, and, on the daily edition, one of the UK's longest-serving environment journalists, Geoffrey Lean, who generally follows a mainstream science approach. The *Daily Telegraph*'s reporting seems to reflect mainstream climate science. Traditionally the *Financial Times* has given little space to sceptical voices in its reporting or opinion columns, although according to the former *FT* environment correspondent, Fiona Harvey, and other observers, this changed significantly in 2010.[231]

As mentioned in Chapter 3, the Boykoff and Mansfield study of

[228] Author interview, June 2011.
[229] 'This Much I Know: James Murdoch, Chairman and CEO, 36, London', *Observer*, 7 June 2009. Kelvin Mackenzie has since moved to the *Daily Mail*.
[230] For details, see www.guardian.co.uk/media/greenslade/2010/jun/21/sundaytimes-scienceofclimatechange.
[231] Author interview, June 2011.

the tabloid press from 2000 to 2006 found that the *Daily Mail* in its reporting demonstrated the greatest percentage of coverage which gave roughly equal attention to competing views regarding humans' role in climate change.[232] Some observers say that, since the period of study, there has been a clearer distinction on the *Mail* between the more mainstream reporting by its environment editor and the frequent space given to sceptical voices in its opinion pages, particularly on policy issues. The *Express* is probably the most explicitly sceptical of all the UK newspapers. It famously ran a front-page story on 15 December 2009 parading '100 Reasons Why Global Warming is Natural',[233] and declares that it has 'led the way' both in exposing the flaws in the arguments supporting global warming and in highlighting public scepticism over the issue. The paper also says that 98% of its readers believe that 'Britons are being conned over man-made global warming theories'.[234]

The *Independent* is proud it was the first Fleet Street newspaper to put a global warming story on its front page (in the late 1990s), and in general its reporting follows the mainstream consensus on climate science. At the time of our survey, Dominic Lawson was a regular columnist on the paper who wrote sceptical pieces. One prominent UK academic has described the *Independent* as having a 'campaigning ethos',[235] an accusation that the paper's science editor, Steve Connor, refutes. He says, 'We did not campaign on climate change. We merely took it very seriously very early on, when other newspapers were still treating it as something of a joke.'[236]

The *Guardian* went through a 'step change' in its coverage of climate change in 2008, according to its head of environment, Damian Carrington. The editors felt the paper's coverage and deployment of resources should reflect the scale of the potential threat to the planet offered by climate change. Since 2008, the paper and online site has had a team of six full-time environment correspondents, two editors, a dedicated picture editor, and two production journalists. In part this was driven by the paper's emphasis on expanding its coverage of the environment on its website. The paper's philosophy was also to avoid putting climate change stories in a special section 'ghetto' but to report throughout the paper on the wider picture of its links to water, energy, food, population, and other related issues.[237]

Figure 6.1 maps the volume of climate change coverage in eight of the ten UK national newspapers (not including the *Star* and the *Financial Times*) from 2000 to 2011. It shows that the *Guardian/Observer* did at times have a larger amount of coverage than other newspapers.

---

[232] Boykoff and Mansfield, 'Ye Olde Hot Aire', 4. The four tabloids studied were the *Sun, Mirror, Express,* and *Mail.*

[233] www.express.co.uk/posts/view/146139/100-reasons-why-global-warming-is-natural.

[234] See e.g. two articles in the paper: Ed Price, 'The Great Climate Change Retreat', 15 Feb. 2010, and Anil Dawar and Will Stewart, 'Climate Change "Lies" by Britain', 17 Dec. 2009.

[235] Mike Hulme, 'Mediated Messages about Climate Change', in Boyce and Lewis (eds), *Climate Change and the Media*, 126.

[236] Author interview, June 2011.

[237] Author interview, June 2011.

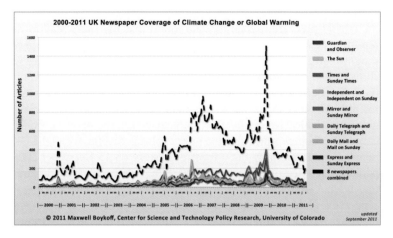

Figure 6.1. UK Newspaper Coverage of Climate Change or Global Warming, 2000–11

However, more importantly, the figure clearly illustrates two peaks in general newspaper coverage in early 2007 and late 2009/2010, which coincide with the two periods of our research.

Methodology and results

The methodology and the research questions applied to the ten UK newspapers[238] are virtually the same as those outlined in Chapter 4. The main difference is that the issue of country differences is not relevant. So the main research questions in the expanded UK study were:

(1) Has there been an increase in the amount of space given to sceptics in the print media of ten UK national newspapers between the two research periods in 2007 and 2009/10?

(2) Are there any important differences between the left-leaning and right-leaning newspapers in the prevalence of sceptical voices?

(3) In which part of a newspaper are sceptical voices most likely to be found?

(4) In broad terms, which types of sceptical voices are most included?

(5) What is the professional background of the sceptics who are quoted?

---

[238] 'Newspapers' is shorthand for the daily and Sunday editions, so references to the *Mail, Mirror, Telegraph, Express, Times, Star*, and *Independent* includes the daily and Sunday editions, unless otherwise specified. The *Sun* does not include its former Sunday stablemate, the *News of the World*.

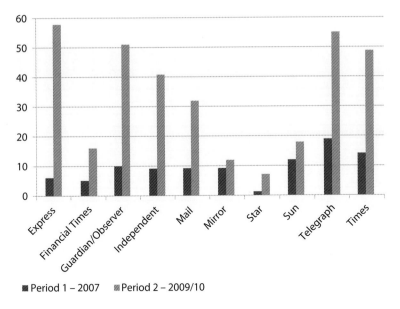

■ Period 1 – 2007   ▨ Period 2 – 2009/10

Figure 6.2. Number of articles of Sceptical Voices in Ten UK National Newspapers, 2007 and 2009/10

Here are the main findings:

The total number of articles found by the search engines in the ten newspapers increased between the three-month period in 2007 (period 1) and the three-month period in 2009/10 (period 2) from 1,270 to 1,558. (See Table 6.2, row 1.) It went up for seven of the papers and declined for three (the *Mail, Mirror,* and *Star*). Those articles 'mentioning' sceptics rose from 94 to 339, a near fourfold increase. (See row 2.) As in Chapter 4, 'mentioning' here includes direct and indirect quotes, generic quotes, and opinion pieces and editorials. In 2007, these represented 7% of all the articles, whereas in 2009/10 this had climbed to 22%.

These numbers mask important differences between the ten newspaper groups. In period 1, the range for the ten newspapers was between 1 article (*Star*) and 19 articles (*Telegraph*) mentioning sceptics. However, in period 2, the range increased to between 7 (*Star*) and 58 (*Express*). The next highest were the *Telegraph* (57), *Guardian* (51), and *The Times* (49). (See Figure 6.2.)

A percentage breakdown is a better guide to how much of their available space newspapers gave to sceptics. (See row 3 of Table 6.2.) In period 1, eight of the newspapers mentioned sceptics in less than 10% of the articles about climate change or global warming in the samples. The two exceptions were the *Telegraph* and the *Sun* (13% each).[239] This was largely due to the presence of sceptical opinion pieces: in the case of the *Sun*, three each from

---

[239] The figures for period 1 in descending order are *Telegraph* and *Sun* (13%), *Mirror* (9%), *Mail* (8%), *Express* and *FT* (7%), *The Times* (6%), *Independent* (5%), *Guardian* and *Star* (4%).

	Express 1	Express 2	Financial Times 1	Financial Times 2	Guardian/Obs 1	Guardian/Obs 2
1. Number of Articles in sample	69	116	74	103	241	313
2. Of which, mentioning sceptics	6	58	5	16	10	51
3. Percentage	7	50	7	16	4	16
Where did articles quoting sceptics appear?						
4. News reports	1	29	3	9	5	35
5. Features	1	1	1	2	1	0
6. Opinion pieces	1	14	0	3	3	11
7. Editorials	2	13	0	2	0	4
8. Reviews	0	0	1	0	1	1
9. Other	1	1	0	0	0	0
Main way sceptical voices included in 4,5,8,9						
10. Direct quotes	2	23	3	9	1	15
11. Indirect quotes	0	0	0	0	6	4
12. Generic	1	8	1	2	0	15
13. Mentioned, not quoted	0	0	1	0	0	2
14. Reviews	0	0	0	0	0	0
15. Other	0	0	0	0	0	0
Main way sceptical voices included in opinion pieces						
16. Author as sceptical scientist	0	0	0	0	0	0
17. Regular columnist expressing sceptical view	1	10	0	0	0	0
18. Invited columnist other than scientist	0	0	0	2	0	2
19. Sceptical voices included but contested	0	4	0	1	3	9
Main way sceptical voices included in editorials						
20. Consensus view seriously contested	1	9	0	0	0	0
21. Tone generally sceptical of measures	1	1	0	0	0	0
22. Sceptical views included but contested	0	3	0	2	0	4
23. Number of sceptics appearing in 10 and 11	6	25	4	14	10	48
24. Number of sceptics appearing in 16-19	0	6	0	2	4	12
	6	31	4	16	14	60
Types of sceptic						
25. Deny global temperatures are warming	0	0	0	2	0	2
26. Anthropogenic contribution over-stated or negligible	6	25	4	11	13	36
27. Serious doubts about impacts or need to combat	0	6	0	3	1	22
28. Science or findings of IPCC seriously flawed	0	0	0	0	0	0
Professional background to sceptics						
29. University scientist	3	7	0	4	4	4
30. Other academic	0	2	0	3	0	7
31. Research group	1	0	0	0	3	0
32. Think tank	0	8	0	5	0	9
33. Amateur	1	4	0	0	3	12
34. Columnist/media	0	4	0	0	1	2
35. Politician/diplomat	1	6	4	4	2	23
36. Business	0	0	0	0	1	1
37. Other	0	0	0	0	0	2
38. Mentions of Lord Lawson	0	3	0	1	3	7
39. Mentions of Benny Peiser	0	1	0	0	0	9

Table 6.2. Prevalence of sceptical voices in 10 UK national newspapers, 2007 and 2009/10

Independent 1	Independent 2	Mail 1	Mail 2	Mirror 1	Mirror 2	Star 1	Star 2	Sun 1	Sun 2	Telegraph 1	Telegraph 2	Times 1	Times 1	Total
17	164	112	66	104	90	24	18	90	117	149	238	230	333	2828
9	41	9	32	9	12	1	7	12	18	19	55	14	49	433
5	25	8	48	9	13	4	39	13	15	13	23	6	15	15
6	25	4	20	5	7	0	5	4	8	5	26	5	26	228
0	0	0	0	1	1	0	0	0	0	2	2	1	2	15
2	10	4	9	2	3	0	0	6	8	10	24	4	17	131
1	5	0	3	1	1	0	2	0	2	1	3	1	2	43
0	1	0	0	0	0	1	0	1	0	1	0	3	0	10
0	0	1	0	0	0	0	0	1	0	0	0	0	2	6
2	15	4	13	3	2	0	3	5	2	7	18	4	9	140
1	3	0	3	0	0	0	0	0	2	0	3	0	9	31
3	8	0	4	3	6	1	2	1	4	1	6	5	11	82
0	0	0	0	0	0	0	0	0	0	0	1	0	0	4
0	0	1	0	0	0	0	0	0	0	0	0	0	0	1
0	0	0	0	0	0	0	0	0	0	0	0	0	1	1
0	0	1	1	1	0	0	0	0	0	2	0	0	0	5
2	1	3	3	1	1	0	0	6	7	2	13	0	3	53
0	2	0	1	0	0	0	0	0	0	2	0	1	2	12
0	7	0	4	0	2	0	0	0	1	4	11	3	12	61
0	0	0	0	0	0	0	0	0	0	0	0	0	0	10
0	0	0	0	0	0	0	1	0	0	0	0	0	0	3
1	5	0	3	1	1	0	1	0	2	1	3	1	2	30
3	34	9	19	3	2	0	3	5	4	12	28	4	28	261
3	10	1	9	1	0	0	0	0	0	10	21	5	16	99
6	44	10	28	4	2	0	3	5	4	22	48	9	44	360
1	1	0	0	0	0	0	0	0	0	0	0	0	0	6
4	19	7	14	3	2	0	3	4	4	19	27	8	25	234
1	24	3	14	1	0	0	0	1	0	3	21	1	19	120
0	0	0	0	0	0	0	0	0	0	0	0	0	0	0
1	2	4	9	1	1	0	2	0	1	9	4	1	2	59
0	1	0	3	0	0	0	0	0	0	0	4	0	5	25
2	4	0	1	0	0	0	0	0	0	5	1	2	0	19
0	3	0	7	0	0	0	0	0	0	2	3	2	8	47
0	3	1	3	1	0	0	0	0	0	2	9	3	9	51
0	4	1	1	0	0	0	1	2	0	1	1	0	3	21
3	27	2	4	1	1	0	0	2	1	2	26	1	15	125
0	0	1	0	1	0	0	0	1	1	1	0	0	1	8
0	0	1	0	0	0	0	0	0	1	0	0	0	1	5
1	10	0	4	0	0	0	0	0	0	0	13	1	13	56
0	5	0	7	0	0	0	0	0	0	0	2	0	3	27

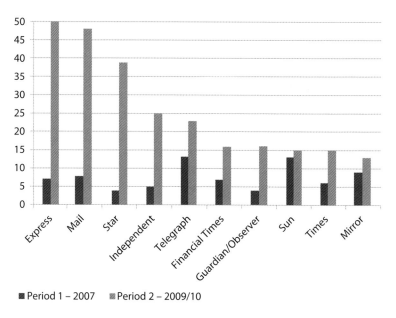

■ Period 1 – 2007　　▨ Period 2 – 2009/10

Figure 6.3. Number of Articles Including Sceptical Voices as % of Total Number of Articles, UK Print Media, 2007 and 2009/10

Kelvin MacKenzie and Jeremy Clarkson, and in the case of the *Telegraph*, ten opinion pieces, six of which expressed strong sceptical views.

In period 2, the percentage figure increased for all ten newspapers, but it was most marked for the *Express, Mail,* and *Star.* (See Figure 6.3.) The *Express* had the most at 50% of all its articles quoting or describing sceptics, followed by the *Mail* (48%) and the *Star* (39%).[240] Six of the newspapers (including all five of the broadsheets and the *Sun*) came in the range between 15 and 25%, whereas the *Mirror* was the only one with less than 15%. Row 3 of Table 6.2 gives the figures for each newspaper.

It is worth mentioning here as we did in Chapter 4 that we did not include in row 2 articles where Rajendra Pachauri or the IPCC were being criticised, if no sceptics were quoted or mentioned within the article. If we had included these articles, the number of articles containing sceptical voices in the *Mail* during period 2 would have increased by 4 to 36, giving it the highest percentage of any paper in our survey (55%).

It is also important to note in which part of the newspaper the sceptical voices were mostly likely to be found. If we do a simple comparison between row 4 of Table 6.2 (news reporting) and row 6 (opinion pieces), and express them both as a percentage of the total number of articles

---

[240] We carried out a limited experiment to see how much difference it would have made to take out from our sample all those articles which the search engine included with 'climate change' or 'global warming' 'at the start', but where in fact the substance of the article was not essentially about those topics. Looking at the second period results for the Express group as an example, of the 48 articles which did not mention sceptics, it was possible to take out 17, thereby reducing the population to 99. (See row 1, Table 6.2.) So, the percentage of articles with sceptical voices would have given a higher figure of 59%, rather than 50%.

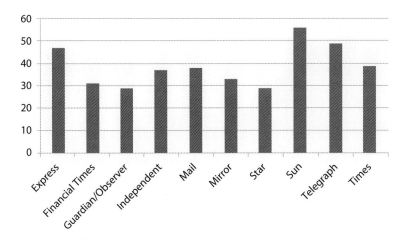

Figure 6.4. Sceptical Voices on Opinion Pages and Editorials as % of All Articles Including Sceptical Voices in UK Print Media, over Two Periods

about climate change including sceptical voices, an interesting picture emerges (for period 2), as seen in Table 6.3.

Table 6.3. News Reports and Opinion Pieces Including Sceptical Voices as % of Total Number of Articles, UK Print Media over Two Periods

	Express	FT	Gdn/Obs	Inde	Mail	Mirror	Sun	Teleg	Times
News reports	50	56	69	61	63	58	44	47	53
Opinion pieces	24	19	22	24	28	25	44	44	35

The first row of the table suggests that left-leaning newspapers (*Guardian, Independent,* and *Mirror*) do seem more likely to have a significantly higher percentage of sceptical voices found in the news reporting than right-leaning newspapers such as the *Sun* and *Telegraph* (although the *Mail* also has a high percentage).[241] Conversely the second row shows that the *Telegraph* and *Sun* have the highest percentage of such voices found in the opinion pages.

A second calculation adding the number of articles found in the two categories of opinion pieces *and* editorials (rows 6 and 7) and expressing it as a percentage of the total number of articles including sceptical voices (row 2) shows that, in period 2, the *Sun* had the highest percentage (56%), followed by the *Telegraph* (49%), the *Express* (47%), *The Times* (39%), and the *Mail* (38%). The other five newspapers fall between 29% and 37%. (See Figure 6.4.) In other words, sceptical voices get a considerable airing in the opinion pieces and editorials of all ten

[241] We have left out the *Star* as it is a small sample.

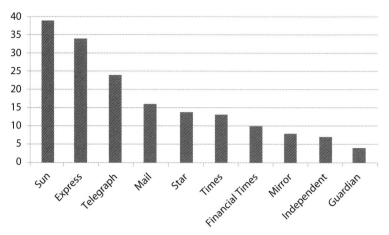

Figure 6.5. Uncontested Sceptical Opinion Pieces or Editorials as % of All Articles in UK Print Media, 2009/10

newspapers, but it tends to be more marked in right-leaning papers.

However, rows 6 and 7 include both opinion pieces where the author mentions sceptical voices but does not necessarily agree with them and editorials where the views of sceptics are included but contested. If these are taken out (rows 19 and 22), then we are left with 'uncontested' pieces where there is no balancing mainstream climate science point of view within the piece. In this case, the percentages drop considerably for most newspapers to below 15%. The exceptions are the *Sun* (39%), the *Express* (34%), the *Telegraph* (24%), and the *Mail* (16%). The remaining percentages are the *Star* 14%, the *FT* 13%, *The Times* 10%, the *Mirror* 8%, the *Independent* 7%, and the *Guardian* 4%. Figure 6.5 clearly shows the lower prevalence in the last three (left-leaning) newspapers of opinion pieces or editorials where sceptical voices are not challenged.

This is one of the most helpful measures in our UK survey of a paper's willingness to give a strong voice to sceptics. In the top four newspapers in the figure (the *Sun, Express, Telegraph,* and *Mail*), there is a strong presence of regular or invited sceptical columnists. In the case of the *Telegraph*, it is Christopher Booker (nine times) and in the case of the *Sun* it is Kelvin MacKenzie (twice), Jeremy Clarkson (twice), and Donald Macleod (twice). In the *Express* and *Mail*, there was a wider range of sceptical voices. In contrast, in the *Mirror* there was only one sceptic in an opinion column over the two periods (Philip Stott, a professor emeritus at SOAS). As mentioned in Chapter 4, the *Guardian* gave space to Benny Peiser and Bjørn Lomborg but as part of wider series of reaction pieces to the Copenhagen summit. The three uncontested pieces in the *Independent* were by Lord Lawson of the GWPF, his son Dominic Lawson, and the Tory MP David Davis.

Another way of measuring the prevalence of sceptical voices is to count the amount of times individual sceptics were quoted directly or indirectly in news and opinion pieces. Row 23 gives these numbers on the news pages for each of the ten newspapers over the two periods.[242] Row 24 gives the number of times they wrote authored pieces or they were quoted or described in opinion pieces written by others.

The total number went up from 80 quotes or mentions in the first period to 280 in the second. All newspapers showed a sharp increase with the exception of the *Mirror* and *Sun* (where the numbers dropped slightly, but from a low base). Top of the list was the *Guardian* where sceptical voices were quoted or described 74 times, followed by the *Telegraph* (70), *The Times* (53), and the *Independent* (50).

As we noted in Chapter 4, it is possible to argue that this growing presence of sceptical voices – even if they are at times included to be argued with or dismissed – can be taken as a sign of increased traction and credibility that such voices were gaining over the period. But it is important to stress that such figures are restricted in their usefulness. First, broadsheet newspapers are very likely to have more mentions of sceptics given the greater column inches available, so it is probably not helpful to compare volume of mentions between broadsheets and tabloids. Second, the figures do not measure in what context these voices are included. In the case of the *Guardian*, for example, the volume of mentions of sceptics was partly driven by the paper's extensive coverage of 'Climategate' in a series of long articles authored by Fred Pearce in the first week of February 2010. Likewise, many of the mentions of sceptics in period 1 found in the *Guardian* and the *Independent* were prompted by discussion of the Channel 4 programme *The Great Global Warming Swindle*.

Thirdly, and most importantly, this coding did not capture whether in the news reporting the mention of sceptics was balanced with other voices, or included in order to be refuted. However, we looked at the news pages of the *Telegraph* in the second period as a limited exercise to test this. An examination of the 28 articles there which included sceptical voices would strongly suggest a high incidence of countervailing voices. If we take out the eight articles in the sample where sceptics were questioning the scientists at the UEA or the IPCC reports, in the remaining 20 articles there were other voices, usually those reflecting mainstream science, in some way balancing those of the sceptics (they varied as to where they appeared in the article, how they were quoted/mentioned, and how often they were quoted/mentioned). Nine of the 20 articles were authored by the *Daily Telegraph* environment correspondent Louise Gray, while the other 11 were written by 'reporters'. This exercise was not applied to other newspapers due to lack of time, but at least in the case of the *Telegraph* group, it would seem that there was a sharp variance between the way sceptical voices appeared in the news pages compared to the 'unchallenged' sceptical views put forward in some of the opinion columns in the same newspaper group.

[242] These numbers do not indicate the number of different sceptics quoted in each newspaper, but the number of times a sceptical voice is quoted. In other words the same sceptic can be quoted several times. It also does not include the times sceptics are just mentioned as individuals (rather than quoted) or the number of times they are quoted generically. See the discussion of methodology in Chapter 4.

Rows 25–28 show the different types of sceptics distinguished according to the categories described above in the coding. There are very few 'outright deniers' that global temperatures are warming, as the Republican senator James Inhofe has been known to argue. However, it is interesting to note that that there are nearly twice as many of the type (ii) sceptics who broadly question the anthropogenic contribution (234), than those who accept it is happening but for different reasons question its impacts or the need to do something about it (120).

It is perhaps significant that of those newspapers where there are large numbers of sceptics mentioned, the *Express* stands out as having a high percentage of type (i) sceptics (31 out of 37, or 84%).

Rows 29–37 show the professional background or affiliation of the sceptics. Of the 360 times individual sceptics were included over the two periods, the largest categories were politicians (125 times), followed by university climate scientists (59), 'amateur' scientists (51), and members of lobby groups or think tanks (47). University climate scientists represented 16% of all sceptical voices quoted or mentioned.

Whereas the number of times university climate scientists were included less than doubled from 23 to 36 between the two periods, the number of times sceptics from think tanks or lobby groups were included increased tenfold (from 4 to 43). A major driver of this was the formation of the GWPF in November 2009. Likewise, 'amateur' sceptics went up fivefold from 11 to 51. Again, a major driver of this was 'Climategate' where sceptics like Steve McIntyre had a strong voice in the media. The number of times sceptical politicians were quoted or mentioned rose from 18 to 107. Their percentage representation went up from 23% to 38%.

There is some evidence for concluding that there were a relatively reduced number of sceptics from universities (rows 29 and 30) who were included a significant number of times. Of the 84 times they were included across the two periods, four of them were quoted or mentioned 10 or more times – Ian Plimer (13 times), Ross McKitrick (11), Bjørn Lomborg (10), and Richard Lindzen (10); one was quoted 6 times (John Christy) and another 5 times (Philip Stott). These six represented 65% of all the times sceptics from universities were included.

A total of 18 university climate scientists were quoted or included (row 29). Seven were from the USA (Lindzen, Christy, Singer, Dyson, Easterbrook, Seitz, Happer), three were from Canada (Clark, Murty, Ball), two from Australia (Plimer, Carter), two from the UK (Stott, Reiter), and one each from Croatia, Sweden, Norway, and Germany.[243] So of the 18 included, 10 were from North America.

It is worth noting the increase in the number of times two senior members of the GWPF were 'mentioned' in the ten newspapers between the two periods. 'Mentioned' here means quoted in news articles,

---

[243] Mojib Latif at the Leibniz Institute was included in the list, but see the discussion of his case in Appendix 3.

described/quoted in opinion pieces written by others or where they themselves were the authors of opinion pieces. Rows 38–39 show that Lord Lawson appeared five times in period 1. This rose to 51 times in the second period (after the GWPF had been formed). Likewise, GWPF director Benny Peiser was not mentioned in the first period but was quoted or described 27 times in the second period. So together, the two went from 5 mentions to 78 mentions over the two periods. In the second period, the two represented 28% of all the times sceptics were quoted or described.

If we just look at the second period, they were most quoted or described (usually quoted) in *The Times* and *Guardian* (16), the *Telegraph* and *Independent* (15), and the *Mail* (11).

The table in Appendix 4 shows the full list of the 52 sceptics who appeared more than once in the ten newspapers. There were 41 other sceptics who were included just once who are not included. A reduced list of those who appeared ten or more times is given in Table 6.4.

Table 6.4 Condensed List of Climate Sceptics

Lord Nigel Lawson	56
Benny Peiser	27
Lord Christopher Monckton	16
Professor Ian Plimer	13
Professor Ross McKitrick	11
Tony Abbott	10
Nigel Calder	10
Professor Bob Lindzen	10
Bjørn Lomborg	10
Steve McIntyre	10
Henrik Svensmark	10

As can be seen, Lord Lawson and Benny Peiser were mentioned or quoted by far the most times over the two periods (although as above, they were mostly quoted in the second period). Plimer, McKitrick, Abbott, Lindzen, Lomborg, and McIntyre have all been described earlier in this study. Nigel Calder is a former editor of the *New Scientist*, who was quoted widely as a result of his participation in the Channel 4 documentary, *The Great Global Warming Swindle*, as was Henrik Svensmark from the Danish Meteorological Institute.

Those listed above were closely followed by Christopher Booker, who was quoted or mentioned nine times, usually by columnists in other newspapers, and by Patrick Michaels (eight times).[244] It is interesting to note that the four sceptics we profiled in Chapter 2 (Monckton, Lomborg, McIntyre, Michaels) were all amongst the most quoted in the UK press. Monckton one would expect, but the three others are not British nor based in the UK. There were only two women sceptics included at all over the two periods out of the total of 93 sceptics: Sarah Palin (three times) and the *Daily Mail* columnist Melanie Phillips (once).

Finally, we chose a period of three months in 2010 (from 1 July to 30 September) after our second period to give an insight into whether the number of sceptics being quoted or mentioned fell off after the initial media interest in 'Climategate' and 'Himalayagate'. Using the same methodology, there were 52 articles in the *Daily* and *Sunday Telegraph* of which 21 – or 40% – included sceptic voices. Of these 21, eight were news articles, nine were opinion pieces or columns, two were features, one was an editorial, and one was an obituary. Of the nine opinion pieces, seven were authored by Christopher Booker. For the *Financial Times* over the same period, the number of articles had dropped to just nine, of which five – or 56% – quoted or described sceptics. A total of nine sceptics (including Benny Peiser twice and Myron Ebell three times) were included in the five articles. So there would seem to be some initial evidence that, even though the total number of articles about climate change or global warming fell off, the percentage with sceptical voices actually *increased* for both the newspapers quite considerably from our second period of research, from 23% to 40% in the case of the *Telegraph*s and from 16% to 56% in the *Financial Times*. However, a longer period or a second period of research would be needed to substantiate these results.

Summary of conclusions

So what can we conclude in answer to our five research questions?

- There was a significant increase in the total amount of articles which contain sceptical voices in all ten UK newspapers between the two research periods in 2007 and 2009/10. The percentage figure (expressed as the number of articles including sceptics as a percentage of the total number of articles about climate change) increased from 7% to 22%, and also increased for all ten newspapers.

- This is not surprising given that the second research period deliberately included 'Climategate' and the questioning of the IPCC. However, what is interesting

---

[244] If we had added Booker's own authored sceptical articles (two in the first period, nine in the second), then he would have come in third place after Benny Peiser with 20 quotes.

is that the percentage increases were much greater for some papers than for others. The *Mail, Express,* and *Star* had both the largest percentage in period 2 (50%, 48% and 39% respectively), and the largest increase between the two periods (43%, 40%, 35% respectively). The *Mirror* had the smallest percentage (13%) and the smallest percentage increase (4%). This would suggest that at least in the case of the tabloids, right-leaning newspapers are more likely to include sceptical voices than left-wing ones.

- A strong correspondence can also be seen between political leaning and propensity to quote or use uncontested sceptical voices in opinion pages and editorials. The top five newspapers with the highest percentage were all right-leaning (the *Sun, Express, Mail, Telegraph,* and *Star* in that order). The three with the smallest percentage (all with less than 10%) were the most left-leaning (the *Mirror, Independent,* and *Guardian*).

- Sceptical voices get a considerable airing in opinion pieces and editorials in all ten newspapers, although it is clearly more marked in some newspapers than others. Expressed as a percentage of the total number of articles mentioning climate change or global warming, the *Sun* had the highest percentage (56%), followed by the *Telegraph, Express, The Times,* and the *Mail.*

- There is evidence from the *Telegraph* newspapers that there is a noticeable difference between the prevalence of uncontested sceptical voices on the news pages compared to the opinion pages. The latter has a much higher incidence.

- Across all ten newspapers, there are nearly twice as many of the 'stronger' type of sceptics who question the anthropogenic contribution, than those who accept it is happening but for different reasons question its impacts or the need to do something about it. The *Express* stands out as having a high percentage of this type of sceptics, whilst the other right-leaning newspapers do not show the same prevalence.

- University climate scientists represented 16% of all sceptical voices quoted over the two periods, compared to 35% for politicians. There was a sharp increase between the two periods monitored in the number of 'amateur' sceptics quoted, and the number of representatives of lobby groups.

- Since its formation, the GWPF has been particularly successful in getting its voice heard across most of the ten newspapers (the exceptions being the *Mirror, Star* and *Sun*). The two sceptics most mentioned or quoted by far in the second period were Lord Lawson and Benny Peiser from the GWPF.

Discussion

A strong correspondence between the political leaning of a newspaper and the prevalence of sceptical voices may not be a surprising result. After all, most of the uncontested scepticism identified in our survey was to be found in the opinion columns of the *Express, Sunday Telegraph, Mail,* and the *Sun* which are often purposefully polemical, one-sided, and (in the case of the first three) representative of a newspaper's ideological preference. That's what helps to sell their newspapers. But it was unexpected that in two right-wing newspapers with a combined daily circulation of 2.7m (the *Express* and the *Mail*), between 48% and 50% of *all* the articles in both the news and opinion pages included sceptical voices. The *Express* in particular stood out: in the post-'Climategate' period, it had the highest percentage of all ten nationals for articles which included sceptical voices, the highest number of sceptical voices included in its news reporting (more than any broadsheet), the highest number of direct quotes from sceptics, the highest number of editorials questioning the mainstream consensus, and the highest number of sceptical opinion pieces of any tabloid.[245]

Academic studies of the UK print media have previously identified that an ideology of a newspaper is a major driver of differences between the general coverage of climate change. As the media academic Anabela Carvalho has written, 'ideology works as a powerful selection device in deciding what is scientific news, i.e. what the relevant "facts" are, and who are the "authorised agents of definition" of science matters'.[246] She showed profound differences between the coverage of *The Times* on the one hand and that of the *Guardian* and the *Independent* on the other in the period 1985–2001. She argued these were in part due to the more conservative ideology of *The Times* and the more social democratic leanings of the *Guardian*, which she described as including values of equity and solidarity, and a sense of global connectedness and global

[245] The paper has been subject to complaints to the Press Complaints Commission about its coverage of global warming, but the PCC has been unable to address them since Jan. 2011 when the paper's owners withdrew its support for the Commission.

[246] Carvalho, 'Ideological Cultures', 223. She defines ideology as 'a set of ideas and values that legitimate a program of action vis-à-vis a given social and political order'.

responsibility. The *Guardian* and *Independent* gave greater importance to the weight of scientific evidence and favoured more state intervention, whereas *The Times* adopted a more liberal, market-oriented view of potential policy options.[247] Similarly, in the Boykoff and Mansfield study of the British tabloids, they write that, in explaining why the *Daily Mail* reflected mainstream climate science the least, 'a key element shaping the difference may be the politically conservative stance of the newspaper, where economic status quo and non-regulatory preferences routinely permeate the editorial pages'.[248]

Our survey would confirm the view that there is a strong correspondence between the political perspective of a British newspaper and the degree of prevalence of sceptical voices. It is worth repeating the statistics: the three left-leaning newspapers (*Guardian, Independent*, and *Mirror*) had the lowest percentages of uncontested editorials and opinion pieces quoting sceptics; between them they had only 10 of the opinion pieces authored by sceptical authors of the total of 70 over the two periods; and that they had no editorials quoting sceptical voices which were left uncontested.

However, all sorts of factors other than ideology impinge on why, how, and where newspapers and journalists decide to include sceptical voices. In our interviews with editors and journalists (or former correspondents) from seven of the ten newspapers included in the survey, different interviewees offered very different perceptions of what shaped their, and their newspapers', decisions on the inclusion of sceptics.[249] These ranged from the strong influence of a newspaper editor (in the case of the *Express* and *Financial Times*), the views of the proprietor (the *Sun*), a heightened awareness of the views and profile of their readers (the *Sun, Express*), the popularity of columnists (the *Sun*), the relevance of sceptics to the particular story they were covering (nearly all of them), to the overarching political perspective of the paper (*Guardian, Mirror,* and *Independent*).

So too simple a reductionism from ideology to prevalence of sceptics is to be avoided. The *Sun* and *The Times* are clearly right-leaning, but by some of the measures used in the analysis above they are more akin to left-leaning newspapers than right-leaning in the prevalence they give to sceptical voices. This clearly marks them out from the media coverage described in Chapter 3 of other parts of the Murdoch media empire in Australia and the USA. This may be partly a result of James Murdoch's influence, but other factors clearly come into play such as the presence of experienced science/environment editors or correspondents, a clear distinction between opinion and news pages, the papers' readership profile and where their ideology stands within the spectrum of right-wing opinion. The two papers broadly support the Cameron

---

[247] As summarised in Hulme, *Why we Disagree about Climate Change*, 223.
[248] Boykoff and Mansfield, 'Ye Olde Hot Aire', 5.
[249] Current or former representatives of the *Guardian, Express, Independent, Telegraph, Mirror, Sun,* and *Financial Times* gave semi-structured interviews. Their answers will form part of a follow-up study. At the time of writing, representatives of the *Mail* and *The Times* were unable or unwilling to take part.

coalition government, which is not climate sceptical. In contrast, many commentators and some editors within other right-leaning media like the *Express* group and the *Sunday Telegraph* question various aspects of Cameron's policies. The two newspapers give considerable space to climate-sceptic voices, which may of course be another way of challenging the Cameron project.

Finally, it is worth stressing that many of the interviewees referred to the way sceptics became a legitimate and more credible part of the story around the time of 'Climategate' and 'Himalayagate'. But some of them also noted that as a result sceptics were emboldened to speak out or be quoted on a wide range of issues around climate change, from the science to the policy of what to do (or not) about combating it. This in large part explains the way organised scepticism, and particularly the GWPF, was able to take advantage of the 'scandals' to reach a remarkably prominent position in the UK print coverage of climate change in the months after its formation.

7. Conclusion

As mentioned in Chapter 1, in July 2011, the Emeritus Professor of Genetics at University College London, Steve Jones, published a far-reaching report on the way the BBC reported three scientific topics, including that of climate science.[250] It criticised the BBC in the following way: 'the climate change deniers have been marginal to the scientific debate but somehow they continued to find a place on the airwaves'. The report gave more oxygen to the debate constantly referred to in this study as to what is an appropriate amount of space for the media to give to sceptics. Some commentators used Professor Jones's report to stress again the distinction between well-established fact and opinion, and the way adversarial dispute on the media may be the best way to cover politics, but not science.[251]

But equally interesting were the divergent ways in which the UK print media reacted to the Jones report. The *Express* headlined its coverage with 'Uproar as BBC Muzzles Climate Change Sceptics', while the *Guardian* headlined its article on the same report 'BBC Gives Too Much Weight to Fringe Views on Issues such as Climate Change'.[252] It seemed proof, if it was needed, of how different newspapers shape their coverage of the same report according to their own underlying perceptions of climate change. What was also of interest was the way parts of the media in the USA and Australia were interested in Professor Jones's report, whereas it seemed to attract little attention elsewhere.[253] Even this small example would seem to confirm a common theme of this study: that climate scepticism is largely an Anglo-Saxon phenomenon both in the media and wider society.

In *Poles Apart*, we have explored the different degrees to which climate scepticism is covered in the media around the world, and the different factors which impinge on the amount and style of coverage. In the UK

[250] www.bbc.co.uk/bbctrust/our_work/other/science_impartiality.shtml.
[251] See e.g. Robin McKie, 'Science and Truth have been Cast Aside by our Desire for Controversy', *Observer*, 24 July 2011.
[252] www.express.co.uk/posts/view/260164/Uproar-as-BBC-muzzles-climate-change-sceptics, and www.guardian.co.uk/science/2011/jul/20/bbc-climate-change-science-coverage.
[253] See e.g. *Climate Progress*, 22 July 2011, wattsupwiththat.com, 23 July 2011, and www.climateshifts.org/?p=6826.

and USA there is strong evidence for seeing a close correspondence between the prevalence of sceptical voices and the political ideology or leaning of a newspaper. These voices, reflecting different types of climate scepticism, are often most manifest in the opinion pages. As we saw in Chapter 5, that is the main explanation for the difference between the *New York Times* and *Wall Street Journal*. The presence on the *WSJ*'s opinion pages of plenty of sceptical voices is consistent with its free-market, pro-business leanings which would oppose strong state intervention or international regulation to deal with climate change.

But it is important to stress that the *WSJ* in its editorial pages often espouses a particular strand of right-wing opinion – a combination of libertarianism and free-market fundamentalism – which is not necessarily the same as more mainstream conservative ideology (which can have strong links to conservation and environmentalism). As we have mentioned before, it is noteworthy that during the period of our research and currently in the UK political party landscape climate scepticism is a minority right-wing view reflected only in the British National Party, UKIP, and on the perimeter of the Conservative Party. Despite powerful sceptical voices on the fringes, the main body of the Conservative Party leadership publicly supports mainstream climate science. This may help to explain why the *Sunday Telegraph* regularly gives space to the columnist Christopher Booker to appeal to disenchanted Conservative and UKIP voters, whilst the *Express*, the most sceptical of all UK newspapers, may also be aiming its coverage at readers with similar views. In contrast, the more mainstream treatment of the science in *The Times* and *Sun*, both of them right-leaning, is more in tune with mainstream Conservative Party thinking.

The view that climate scepticism is mainly a feature of a certain narrow strand of conservative ideology (libertarian and strongly free-market) may also help to explain the situation in the USA where the Republican Party leadership is heavily influenced by the climate-sceptical, libertarian, and free-market Tea Party. As we mentioned in Chapter 2, there is evidence that Tea Party supporters are the most climate-sceptical group of all political groupings: they say global warming is either naturally caused (50%) or is not happening at all (21%).[254] They are also more politically conservative than Republicans, Democrats, and Independents, more likely to be 'born-again' or evangelicals, less likely to believe that humans evolved from earlier species of animals, and more likely to hold relatively anti-egalitarian views.

This is also one factor explaining the *absence* of persistent climate-sceptic voices in the media in Brazil, France, and India: there are no conservative parties or significant elements within them who energetically follow that type of conservative ideology whom the (right-leaning) print media can quote. It can be no coincidence that in those three countries divergences in the political leanings of newspapers did

[254] See n. 62.

not seem to be drivers of differences in coverage of climate scepticism to anything like the extent found in the USA and the UK. It is also significant that, as we saw in Chapter 4, it was in the UK and the US print media that politicians were extensively quoted, in sharp contrast to the media in Brazil, France, and India.

However, there may be a danger in over-stating the role of ideology. The individual country studies suggest that outcomes are usually determined by the interaction between internal processes or factors within newspapers (such as journalistic practices, editorial culture, or the influence of editors and proprietors as well as political ideology) and external societal forces (such as the power or presence of sceptical lobbying groups, sceptical scientists, sceptical political parties, or sceptical readers who are simply fearful of higher taxes or energy bills). An array of other factors, such as a country's energy profile, the presence of web-based scepticism, and a country's direct experience of a changing climate also play a role. In Chapter 2 we suggested ways in which USA society is exceptional, while in the UK a highly competitive tabloid culture with a strong political or quasi-campaigning agenda clearly plays a large part. In Brazil, factors that seem to be important are a strong tradition of trained science journalists, the absence of organised lobby groups linked to the fossil fuel industry, and the virtual absence of strongly sceptical voices in the elite scientific, political, and business community. In China, scepticism is absent from the media largely because the press follows the official line on climate science, while in India the absence of business-linked lobby groups, the presence of strong environmental NGOs, the dominant framing of the issue in the media as a nationalistic 'us-versus-them' narrative, and the paucity of climate-sceptical scientists, all play a part. In France, some of these factors also have a role, but a strong 'pro-science' or rationalist culture in wider French society is probably an additional prism through which to evaluate the experience of reporting climate change there.

This last observation points to one of the weaknesses of this study. The way in which climate scepticism feeds into, and is a manifestation of, wider anti-science sentiments both within a newspaper and wider society is just one area which needs further research. As a corollary of this, a tradition of environmentalism in some (European) countries or media may provide a stronger antidote to climate scepticism than in the USA. Another area is how climate scepticism on the internet plays out in different countries, and the ways it can set an agenda, influence newspaper editors, or be part of a general editorial or business proposition for a newspaper. The degree to which a journalist in a developing country may be influenced by direct experience of the climate changing or more extreme weather is another. Or the extent to which weather extremes are a *shared* experience in the same country may be significant. As Andy Revkin has pointed out about the USA,

113

even when Hurricane Katrina swamped New Orleans,
it didn't affect the country's economy, it didn't cause a
recession, it was a few thousand people in a famous city but
a place that most people hadn't been to. So there's something
about the size and breadth of the country that does get in
the way of having a consensus.[255]

All these topics deserve further investigation. However, in conclusion, the weight of this study would suggest that, out of this wide range of factors, the presence of politicians espousing some variation of climate scepticism, the existence of organised interests that feed sceptical coverage, and partisan media receptive to this message, all play a particularly significant role in explaining the greater prevalence of sceptical voices in the print media of the USA and the UK. Expressed at its simplest level, journalists are going to quote politicians and lobbyists who are sceptical of climate change if they are there to be quoted. The fact that such politicians or groups are largely absent or have a reduced presence in Brazil, China, France, and India goes a long way to explaining why climate scepticism is not so prevalent in the print media in these countries (even though in three of the countries, there is a politically divided newspaper landscape).

This study has gone to some lengths to describe the full spectrum of climate scepticism. This is because we think, like many other commentators, that it is the role of good journalism to differentiate between the types of scepticism.[256] Climate change is a multifaceted subject, but all too often different types of sceptics are grouped together when they are of very different hues. In particular, it seems important to label whether climate sceptics are of the type who question the science, or of the type who question which mitigation policies or technologies are the most appropriate – in other words, what exactly are they sceptical about? It seems also important to make clear where there is consensus and where there is not about which aspects of the science, and to reflect on what is a proportionate and appropriate amount of coverage for the different sceptical viewpoints. As we have mentioned, there is a great deal of scientific debate about the timing, location, and extent of impacts, but much less about the significant role that man-made GHGs play in warming global temperatures. The Broadcasting Code which requires all UK broadcasters, including the BBC, to show '*due*

---

[255] Interview with author, July 2011. Hurricane Katrina apparently caused a swing away from climate scepticism, but it was only temporary.

[256] For a detailed discussion of these issues within the US media, see the pieces authored by Curtis Brainard at Columbia Journalism Review's *The Observatory*: 'Finding the Right Expert' on 29 June 2010, 'Making Space for Experts' on 3 Apr. 2009, 'Quashing Climate Dissent?' 14 Aug. 2008, and 'The Skeptics Ball', 4 Mar. 2008. General guides for journalists on covering climate change can be found at Tom Yulsman,'7 Tips for Covering Climate Change': www.poynter.org/uncategorized/99830/7-tips-for-covering-climate-change; News University's online course, 'Covering Climate Change': www.newsu.org/courses/covering-climate-change; and L. Jeremy Richardson and Bud Ward (eds), 'Reporting on Climate Change: Understanding the Science', Environmental Law Institute, 2011. In the UK the International Institute for Environment and Development (IIED) regularly publishes guides and tips for journalists, whilst Professor Jones' report for the BBC carries discussion on the issues, in pp. 66–72.

impartiality' seems particularly appropriate here.[257] So clear signposting by journalists can go some way to help public understanding, as can clear indications of whether an interviewee represents a minority view and what he or she has published in the field being discussed. On the strength of this piece of research, it is also constantly worth testing whether the general political perspective of a newspaper, organisation, or journalist can become too dominant a force in shaping the coverage to the point of being an obstacle to better treatment of the issue. After all, global warming is too important a topic, with potentially far-reaching consequences, to let a prior political perspective get in the way of the search for greater understanding about the way the natural world works.

More clarity about the motivations for scepticism, and whether it is more about the science or about the perceived policy implications, could help to reduce the polarisation of the way the public, politicians, and the media view the issue of climate change. As the veteran British environment journalist Geoffrey Lean has argued, despite the often vitriolic debate, there is probably more common ground than many would expect. 'All but the extremists on either side agree that the planet is warming and that humanity is at least partly responsible – and that we don't know how big its contribution is, or what the effects will be,' he writes.

> Of course, it's much harder to reach conclusions in this area than on the basic science. So we are clearly embroiled in the wrong argument. We should be debating not scientific certainty, but risk – or, more precisely, what levels of risk we are prepared to take with the futures of our children and grandchildren.[258]

---

[257] According to the BBC guidelines, 'the term "due" means that the impartiality must be adequate and appropriate to the output, taking account of the subject and nature of the content, the likely audience expectation and any signposting that may influence that expectation. Due impartiality is often more than a simple matter of "balance" between opposing viewpoints ...' See www.bbc.co.uk/editorialguidelines/page/guidelines-impartiality-introduction. In contrast, under the PCC's code of conduct, UK newspapers are free to be partisan. Hence, if a UK newspaper interprets climate change science as a political issue, it can invoke the right to cover different opinions. This can been seen in a recent PCC ruling which said newspapers are only obliged to report views accurately, not to ensure that the views themselves are accurate: www.pcc.org.uk/cases/adjudicated.html?article=NjE4OQ==.
[258] Geoffrey Lean, 'How Much Risk can we Take with Life?', *Daily Telegraph*, 13 Feb. 2010.

Appendix 1: 'Climategate'

The controversy known as 'Climategate' broke on 20 November 2009, just days before the 15th round of climate change negotiations in Copenhagen known as COP-15 under the auspices of the UNFCCC. More than 3,000 documents and over 1,000 private emails appeared online that were exchanges between the Climatic Research Unit (CRU) at the University of East Anglia (UEA) in the UK and climate scientists outside the Unit. The UEA alleges that the emails and documents were illegally hacked. Various allegations have been made about the perpetrators of the hacking (or of the possible leaking), ranging from foreign intelligence agencies to lobbyists in the USA, but at the time of writing it was still not known who was responsible and a police investigation was still ongoing.

The emails discussed sensitive topics such as difficulties in presenting evidence for anthropogenic global warming, and expressions of the scientists' desires and strategies to avoid granting some of their critics scientific legitimacy or access to their data. Climate sceptics claimed the emails showed that UEA scientists had manipulated and suppressed key climate data. For example, amongst the quotes found in the emails was a comment by Professor Phil Jones, director of the CRU, to Professor Mike Mann of the University of Virginia in 1999. In it Professor Jones discussed using 'Mike's Nature trick' to 'hide the decline'. The phrase was widely quoted by politicians like James Inhofe in the US to mean that scientists were trying to prevent the truth getting out that global temperatures had stopped rising. However, the UEA scientists explained that the 'decline' referred to a drop in temperatures inferred from the proxy analysis of tree rings, and that the 'trick' meant a graphic device to merge different sets of data from tree rings and thermometer readings.

There were numerous independent investigations into 'Climategate', including one by the UK House of Commons Science and Technology Committee and two by independent committees commissioned by the UEA that focused on the science being done at CRU (led by Lord Oxburgh) and on the behaviour of the scientists involved (led by Sir Russell Muir). These largely exonerated the scientists, finding no evidence of deliberate scientific malpractice. However, the investigations criticised aspects of their behaviour, including their lack of full transparency over sharing the data supporting their scientific findings and their efforts to exclude the work of certain scientists in peer-reviewed journals and assessments. For example, the Muir Report concluded that 'their rigour and honesty as scientists are not in doubt', but it added that 'there has been a consistent pattern of failing to display the proper degree of openness', notably over complying with Freedom of Information requests. The CRU scientists were too quick to dismiss critics from outside their own circles, the report added. Some climate sceptics said that the reports did not bring 'Climategate' to an end, as they were superficial or lacking in balance.

Appendix 2: Research Coding Sheet

1. Name of researcher: ....

Country: ....

publication ....

2. Period under research:

....
Search engine, search words and search options used:

....

3. a) Number of articles found: .... ; b) when repeats, letters and 'trails' removed: .... c) of which, number in which sceptical voices are included: ....

4. Of the number above in 3) c), in which parts of the newspaper did they appear:

      a) News reports: ....

      b) Features: ....

      c) Opinion pieces/columns: ....

      d) Editorials: ....

      e) Reviews (film, TV, book): ....

      f) Other: ....

5. Which of the following categories was the main way sceptical voices were included in the articles:

a) News reports/Features/Reviews/Other:

i) where named, individual sceptics were quoted directly: ....

ii) where named, individual sceptics were quoted indirectly: ....

iii) where individual sceptics were not named, but sceptical voices were quoted or described generically (e.g. 'sceptics say that…'): ....

iv) where the names of individual sceptics are mentioned as part of a report, although they are not quoted: ....

v) where sceptical vox pops (i.e. non-specialists) were used: ....

vi) Other: ....

b) Opinion pieces:

i) where the author is a scientist, expressing essentially a sceptical view: ....

ii) where the author is not a scientist but a regular columnist, expressing essentially a sceptical view: ....

iii) where the author is not a scientist, but an invited columnist (e.g. politician etc), expressing essentially a sceptical view: ....

iv) where the author includes sceptical view points, but either disputes them, rejects them or does not agree with them: ....

c) Editorials:

i) where the consensus on climate change science is seriously questioned: ....

ii) where the tone is in general sceptical of measures to combat climate change: ....

iii) where the views of sceptics are included, but where their views are disputed or rejected, or where the conclusions are measured: ....

6. For each of the articles identified under 5) a) i) – ii), please list (on a separate sheet) the names of the sceptics mentioned (sample as below):

Article date:	Name of Sceptic:	Category under 8) below;	Category under 9) below:
Feb 3/2007	John Smith	ii) b)	i)
Feb 5/2007	Richard Lindzen	iii) a)	i)

etc.

Total number of different sceptical voices quoted in news articles:
....

7. For each of the articles under 5) b) i) – iv), please list (on a separate sheet) the names of the sceptics mentioned:

Total number of different sceptical voices quoted in opinion pieces:
....

8. **Types of sceptic:** For each of the named sceptics mentioned in 6) and 7) above, to the best of your knowledge, assign them to one of the following categories:

i) global temperatures are not warming: ....

ii) global temperatures are warming, but a) the anthropogenic contribution (burning fossil fuels) to global warming or climate change is over-stated, negligible, or non-existent compared to other factors like natural variations or sun spots: ....

Or b) it is not known with any or enough certainty what the main causes are: ....

iii) Anthropogenic global warming is happening, but

> a) it is not known with enough certainty what the impacts will be, due to inadequacies of climate modelling or other doubts (e.g. Richard Lindzen: 'we are not in a position to forecast what the climate will be the future … initial warming could unleash negative feedbacks that will dampen down temperature'): ....

> b) urgent action by governments and/or substantial government spending (on all or some aspects of mitigation or adaptation) to counter AGW is not necessary (e.g. short-term costs are too high, some parts of the world could benefit, the response is disproportionate to the threat, the impacts are too uncertain etc): ....

c) the science or findings of the IPCC reports are seriously
flawed: ....
iv) other: ....

9. Main professional background or affiliation of sceptic:

i) university scientist (e.g. Richard Lindzen)

ii) academic tied to university but not a scientist (e.g. Bjørn Lomborg)

iii) non-university based research organisation (e.g. NASA)

iv) think tank or lobbying group (e.g. the Global Warming Policy
Foundation in the UK)

v) 'amateur' scientist with no affiliation to i) to iv) above (e.g. Steve
McIntyre)

vi) newspaper columnist or media personality (e.g. Christopher
Booker)

vii) politician or diplomat (e.g. James Inhofe)

viii) business sector

ix) other

Appendix 3: Methodology – Issues and Limitations

Several issues arose out of the coding. First, and importantly, the search engines came up with significant numbers of articles where the key words 'climate change' or 'global warming' were mentioned briefly at the start but where the main focus of the article was not about either of these topics. Examples of this were, for instance, where a feature on a personality would mention at the start that he or she was interested in climate change, or where a columnist would have a long list of complaints that included climate change, but where the article did not proceed to delve into the topic. We decided to keep these in the sample, while recognising that, if we had taken them out, in some cases the percentage figures expressed in rows 3 of Tables 4.1 and 6.2 would have been considerably higher.

A second issue was that sceptical voices could appear in several ways in an article, as described in part 5) of the coding sheet, but we opted for the main way they appeared. This usually meant that if a sceptical voice was directly or indirectly quoted, the article would be categorised under (5)(i)a or (5)(i)b.

The next issue was that an opinion piece could be sceptical in tone about global warming/climate change or the need to take measures to combat it, but include no mention or quoting of sceptical voices. These were generally excluded. There were several articles, particularly in the UK press, about 'Climategate' and specifically the problems with the IPCC reports or attacking the IPCC or its chairman, Rajendra Pachauri, where no sceptical voices were mentioned or quoted. For example, there were several articles in the *Daily/Sunday Telegraph* and the *Mail* criticising the IPCC and its chair, which ended up not being included as articles with sceptical voices in them, even though the general tenor of the articles may have left the reader questioning the edifice of mainstream climate science. We did not add these to our number of articles with sceptics in them. Again, the percentage figures would have been higher if we had.

Another difficult issue was how wide to cast the net of what type of sceptics to include. The full list and categories can be seen in part 8 of the coding sheet. However, this still left open what sort of sceptics should be included under each of the categories. For example, we opted not to include sceptics who argue that biofuels should not be part of the solution to reducing GHGs, or sceptics who question whether China will ever be able to reduce significantly its GHGs whilst it is committed to building more coal-fired generators. In the first case, it would have meant including figures like Fidel Castro, who is hardly known as a sceptic about global warming, and in the second case, it would have cast the net of scepticism even wider.

A more knotty problem was that a particular sceptic may be best known for his (and it is virtually always a man) particular type of scepticism, but he might appear in an article voicing a different type of scepticism. An example of this is Richard Lindzen, from the Massachusetts Institute of Technology, who is widely regarded as the most serious scientist of the sceptics and is probably best known for his view that 'CO_2 will harm the planet, but believes that the initial warming will unleash negative feedbacks that will damp it down'.[259] But he has also been quoted where he appears to be denying that anthropogenic global warming is happening.[260] Another problem is that a sceptic could change his position over time, which appears to be the case with Bjørn Lomborg and Tony Abbott.[261] Or a sceptic could chop and change their main argument. Yet another problem is that a scientist could be quoted or described as a sceptic in an article, but later denies or clarifies that he did not agree with this categorisation. A case in point is Mojib Latif from the Leibniz Institute, who was quoted in the *Mail on Sunday* and *Star* in the UK and described as a sceptic, but who later clarified to the *Guardian* that he was not.[262] Roger Pielke is another who is often quoted in the media as a sceptic but rejects such a label.[263]

Another challenge was that a sceptic could articulate both type (ii) and type (iii) of scepticism within the same article. After all, most sceptics who believe in type (ii) – that broadly speaking, the anthropogenic contribution to global warming is over-stated – are likely to believe also in type (iii): broadly, there is no need for drastic cuts in fossil fuel emissions. In this case, we opted to include them as type (ii) sceptics.

We also decided to assign to each sceptic one coding category across all countries for the sake of consistency, which we chose on the basis of how the sceptic was best known. In the case of Mojib Latif, we included him in the list of sceptics when he appeared in the UK's *Daily Mail* and *Daily Star*, as a reader would have interpreted him as such.

Finally, in part 9 it was at times difficult to assign some of the

[259] Pearce, *Climate Files*, 80.
[260] Boykoff, 'Public Enemy No. 1?', 5.
[261] See Juliette Jowit, 'Bjørn Lomborg: $100bn a Year Needed to Fight Climate Change', *Guardian*, 30 Aug. 2010. For Tony Abbott, see Clive Cookson, 'Backlash by Sceptics Gains Grounds After "Climategate"', *Financial Times*, 5 Dec. 2009.
[262] See David Adam, 'Leading Climate Scientist Challenges Mail on Sunday's Use of his Research', *Guardian*, 11 Jan. 2010.
[263] Larson and Keating, 'The FP Policy Guide to Sceptics'.

sceptics to one category as many 'crossed over' between an affiliation to, for example, a university and a think tank. Lord Lawson in the UK is a politician, but also the founder and a very active member of the GWPF. We therefore had to make a judgement on the main affiliation of the sceptic. It should also be clarified that the category of 'newspaper columnist or media personality' refers to the times these were quoted in other articles – the numbers did not include the opinion pieces authored by themselves (this would have been captured in part (5)(b) (ii) of the coding sheet).

The limitations of the methodology

The above discussion implies a number of obvious limitations to interpreting the results emerging out of the coding sheets. The main ones are:

1. This piece of research was mainly quantitative, not qualitative, in the sense that it was essentially counting the number and type of sceptical voices appearing in the different categories of articles. The coding was designed to suggest answers to the key research questions posited at the beginning of Chapters 4 and 6. For example, it did not attempt to capture how each news report under (5)a would have fitted the three categories commonly used for assessing the portrayal of climate change issues, as discussed above in Chapter 3: the 'consensus view' (climate change is real and human-caused), 'falsely balanced view' (we don't know if climate change is real, or if humans are a cause), and the 'dismissive view' (climate change is not happening, or there is no role for humans).

   In other words, it did not set out to establish the overall tenor of a news report and did not distinguish whether the inclusion of sceptical voices was left unchallenged by voices who accept the mainstream science on climate change, or who argue that urgent measures need to be adopted to combat the possible effect of GHGs. Likewise, although the coding went some way to capturing the portrayal of climate change in the opinion pieces and editorials, it excluded from the coding all those articles in those two categories where no sceptical voices were included. So, for example, it could have been the case that the majority of all the articles mentioning climate change or global warming in a newspaper in one of the periods, even though they included many articles with climate sceptic voices in them, strongly reflected the mainstream view on the science of climate change.

However, we would argue that (a) the coding was 'fit for purpose' to address the research questions outlined above; (b) measuring the presence of sceptical voices is a good indicator of how much presence – and therefore arguably traction and credibility – they acquired over the two periods in question; (c) the coding chosen does not undermine the validity of within country and cross-country comparisons as the same criteria were applied across all the sample articles; and (d) the different categorisation of the opinion pieces and editorials does offer useful insights into how different newspapers treated sceptical voices.

2. The exclusion of online articles from the sample period was clearly restrictive. For example, James Delingpole, a well-known and outspoken sceptic on the *Telegraph* website, did not appear in our sample in the print version of the paper, but clearly he is a significant sceptic voice in the UK. Likewise, many comment pieces by regular columnists do not make into the print version. Moreover, important articles quoting sceptics such as the *Daily Mail*'s online news report on 15 February 2010 (falling within the second period) did not appear in the print version, and so did not appear in our sample.[264] In the report, the business tycoon Donald Trump called for the former US vice-president Al Gore to be stripped of his Nobel Peace Prize because of the record-breaking snowstorms in the US.

3. The position of an article in the paper could clearly make a huge difference as to its potential impact on a reader, and indeed, the likelihood of their reading it. So for example, the *Daily Express*'s front-page splash on 15 December 2009, '100 Reasons Why Global Warming is Natural' would leave a clearer message than if it had been tucked away in the middle of the paper.

4. At least in the case of the UK media, the lack of a breakdown between Sunday and daily editions of the newspaper may have been an obstacle to a more

---

[264] www.dailymail.co.uk/news/article-1251283/Donald-Trump-Climate-campaigner-Al-Gore-stripped-Nobel-Peace-Prize-record-snow-storms.html.

nuanced set of results. For example, some of the people interviewed for this study said there was a significant difference between the *Telegraph* and *Sunday Telegraph* – the latter has often been viewed as more ideologically driven than its daily counterpart. The *Sunday Telegraph* has a regular sceptical columnist, Christopher Booker, while the *Daily Telegraph* has the veteran environment correspondent Geoffrey Lean, whose columns mainly reflect mainstream consensus. Moreover, the editorial dynamic of Sunday newspapers is often different as opinion-driven, in-depth features, less tied to the daily news agenda, are more prevalent.

5. Finally, as mentioned above, we did not include in our category of articles with sceptical voices those articles or opinion pieces which were essentially critical of the IPCC or of its chair, Rajendra Pachauri, but where no sceptical voices were mentioned or quoted. If we had done so, the results for the Telegraph group for example, would have gone up to a total of 62 (an increase of 5) in period 2, which would have meant that it would have overtaken the Express group as having the largest number of articles with sceptical voices of any newspaper in our study.

Appendix 4. List of Sceptics 'Mentioned' More than Once in Ten UK National Newspapers

		No. of mentions
Tony Abbott	Leader Liberal Party, Australia	10
Joe Barton	Republican congressman, USA	3
David Bellamy	TV presenter, UK	2
Godfrey Bloom	UKIP MEP, UK	2
Christopher Booker	*Sunday Telegraph* columnist, author, UK	9
Nigel Calder	Former editor *New Scientist* (1962–6), author, UK	10
Bob Carter	Prof, Marine geologist, James Cook Uni, Queensland Australia	3
Ian Clark	Prof, Earth Sciences, Uni Ottawa, USA	2
John Christy	Prof, Atmospheric Science, Uni Alabama, USA	6
Piers Corbyn	Forecaster, Weather Action, UK	2
David Davis	Conservative MP, UK	7
Martin Durkin	TV producer, UK	2
Freeman Dyson	Prof, Physics, Princeton Uni, USA	2
Don Easterbook	Emeritus Prof, Geologist, Western Washington Uni, USA	2
Myron Ebell	Competitive Enterprise Institute, USA	2
Eigil Friis-Christensen	Prof, Director of the Danish National Space Centre, Denmark	5
Nick Griffin	Leader, British National Party, UK	8
Roger Helmer	Conservative MEP, UK	2
David Holland	Retired engineer, Northampton, UK	7
James Inhofe	Republican senator, USA	5
Douglas Keenan	Former City banker, UK	2

Vaclav Klaus	President, Czech Republic	4
Lord Nigel Lawson	Politician, author, chairman of the GWPF, UK	56
Steven Levitt and Stephen Dubner	Authors of *Freakonomics* and *Superfreakonomics*, USA	2
Richard Lindzen	Prof of Meteorology, MIT, Boston, USA	10
Martin Livermore	Author, Director of the Scientific Alliance UK, UK	2
Bjørn Lomborg	Author, adjunct Professor Copenhagen Business School, Denmark	10
Jim McConalogue	Political analyst, European Foundation, UK	2
Stephen Mcintyre	Ex-minerals prospector, editor climateaudit.org, Canada	10
Ross McKitrick	Prof, Univ of Guelph, fellow of Fraser Institute, Canada	11
Patrick Michaels	Senior fellow, Cato Institute, and Prof, Uni of Virginia, USA	8
Lord Christopher Monckton	UKIP, author, UK	16
Andrew Montford	Author, runs blogsite, Bishop Hill, UK	2
Tim Montgomerie	Editor of Conservative Home website, UK	2
Patrick Moore	Current chair, Greenspirit strategies, Vancouver, Canada	2
Richard North	Dr, blogger, author, UK	5
Michael O'Leary	CEO, Ryanair, Ireland	5
Vladimir Paar	Physicist, Zagreb Uni, Croatia	2
Sarah Palin	Republican politician, USA	3
Benny Peiser	Director, GWPF, UK	27
Ian Plimer	Prof, Geologist, Uni of Adelaide, Australia	13
John Redwood	Conservative MP, UK	4
Paul Reiter	Prof, Entomology, Pasteur Institute in Paris, France	3
Craig Rucker	Director, Committee for a Constructive Tomorrow, USA	2
Mohammad Al-Sabban	Head of delegation at the Copenhagen summit, Saudia Arabia	3
Tom Segelstad	Dr, Geochemist, University of Oslo, Norway	2
Fred Singer	Emeritus Prof, Physicist, Uni of Virginia, USA	2
Philip Stott	Emeritus Prof of biogeography, SOAS, UK	5
Henrik Svensmark	Danish Meteorological Institute, Denmark	10
Peter Taylor	Author, UK	2
Alan Titchmarsh	TV presenter, UK	2
Anthony Watts	Radio weatherman, blogger, Watts Up With That, USA	6
Xie Zhenhua	Delegate to UN, China	3

Acronyms and Abbreviations

ABC	Australian Broadcasting Corporation
AGW	Anthropogenic Global Warming
BBC	British Broadcasting Corporation
BNP	British National Party
CERES	Creative Responses to Sustainability
CJR	Columbia Journalism Review
CNN	Cable News Network
CPR	Centre for Policy Research (India)
CRU	Climatic Research Unit (part of the UEA)
EPA	Environmental Protection Agency (USA)
FAIR	Fairness and Accuracy in Reporting
FT	*Financial Times*
GHG	Greenhouse Gas
GWPF	Global Warming Policy Foundation
IPCC	Intergovernmental Panel on Climate Change
NASA	National Aeronautics and Space Administration
NCDC	National Climatic Data Center
NYT	*New York Times*
PCC	Press Complaints Commission
RISJ	Reuters Institute for the Study of Journalism
TOI	*Times of India*

UCS   Union of Concerned Scientists

UEA   University of East Anglia

UKIP   UK Independence Party

UNFCCC   United Nations Framework Convention on Climate
          Change

WSJ   *Wall Street Journal*

Bibliography

General

TAMMY BOYCE and JUSTIN LEWIS (eds), *Climate Change and the Media* (New York: Peter Lang, 2009).

MAXWELL T. BOYKOFF, 'Flogging a Dead Norm? Newspaper Coverage of Anthropogenic Climate Change in the United States and United Kingdom from 2003 to 2006', *Area*, 39/4 (2007).

— (ed.), *The Politics of Climate Change* (London and New York: Routledge, 2010).

— 'Public Enemy No. 1? Understanding Media Representations of Outlier Views on Climate Change', *American Behavioral Scientist* (2011), 5.

— *Who Speaks for the Climate? Making Sense of Media Reporting on Climate Change* (Cambridge, Cambridge University Press, 2011).

— and J. BOYKOFF, 'Balance as Bias: Global Warming and the US Prestige Press', *Global Environmental Change*, 15/4 (2004), 125–36.

— and MARIA MANSFIELD, '"Ye Olde Hot Aire": Reporting on Human Contributions to Climate Change in the UK Tabloid Press', *Environmental Research Letters*, 3 (2008).

ANABELA CARVALHO, 'Ideological Cultures and Media Discourses on Scientific Knowledge: Re-Reading News on Climate Change', *Public Understanding of Science*, 16 (2007), 223–43.

RILEY E. DUNLAP and AARON M. MCCRIGHT, 'Climate Change Denial: Sources, Actors and Strategies', in *Routledge Handbook of Climate Change and Society* (London: Routledge, 2010), ch. 14.

NEIL GAVIN and TOM MARSHALL, 'Mediated Climate Change in Britain: Scepticism on the Web and on Television around Copenhagen', *Global Environmental Change*, 21 (2011), 1035–44.

GREENPEACE, *Dealing in Doubt: The Climate Denial Industry and Climate Science* (Amsterdam: Greenpeace International, 2010).

JAMES HOGGAN, *Climate Cover-Up: The Crusade to Deny Global Warming* (Vancouver: Greystone Books, 2009).

MIKE HULME, *Why we Disagree about Climate Change* (Cambridge: Cambridge University Press, 2009).

AARON M. MCCRIGHT and RILEY E. DUNLAP, 'The Politicization of Climate Change and Polarization in the American Public's Views of Global Warming, 2001–2010', *Sociological Quarterly*, 52/2 (2011), 155–94.

GEORGE MONBIOT, *Heat: How to Stop the Planet Burning* (London: Penguin, 2006).

MATTHEW NISBET, *Climate Shift: Clear Vision for the Next Decade of Public Debate*, American University School of Communication, 2011.

NAOMI ORESKES and ERIK CONWAY, *The Merchants of Doubt: How a Handful of Scientists Obscured the Truth on Issues from Tobacco Smoke to Global Warming* (New York: Bloomsbury Press, 2010).

JAMES PAINTER, *Summoned by Science: Reporting Climate Change at Copenhagen and Beyond* (Oxford: Reuters Institute for the Study of Journalism, 2010).

FRED PEARCE, *The Climate Files: The Battle for the Truth about Global Warming* (London: Guardian Books, 2010).

HAYDN WASHINGTON and JOHN COOK, *Climate Change Denial: Heads in the Sand* (London: Earthscan, 2011).

Brazil

RICHARD J. LADLE, ANA CLAUDIA MENDES MALHADO, PETER A. TODD, and ACACIA C. M. MALHADO, 'Perceptions of Amazonian Deforestation in the British and Brazilian Media', *Acta Amazonica*, 40/2 (2010), 319–24.

ANDI, 'Climate Change in the Brazilian News Media', 2009: http://www.mudancasclimaticas.andi.org.br/pdf/analise_media_mc_eng.pdf

China

SAM GEALL, 'Climate-Change Journalism in China: Opportunities of International Cooperation', *chinadialogue* (London, 2011).

HONGYANG GOU, 'Low-Carbon Plot', *Shanxi Economic Press* (2010).

SANDY TOLAN, *Coverage of Climate Change in Chinese Media* (UN Human Development Report, Occasional Paper, 2007).

France

C. A. D. D. M. ALLÈGRE, *L'imposture climatique ou la fausse écologie* (Paris: Plon, 2010). Benson, R., 'La Fin du Monde? Tradition and Change in the French Press', *Culture and Society*, 22/1 (2004), 108–26.

P. CHAMPAGNE, 'L'Environnement, les risques et le champ journalistique', *Regards sociologiques*, 14 (1997), 73–90.

J.-B. COMBY, 'Quand l'environnement devient «médiatique»: Conditions et effets de l'institutionnalisation d'une spécialité journalistique', *Réseaux*, 157–8 (2009), 159–90.

S. FOUCART, *Le Populisme climatique: Claude Allègre and Cie, enquête sur les ennemis de la science* (Paris: Denoël Impacts, 2010).

R. KUHN, *The Media in Contemporary France* (Buckingham: Open University Press, 2011).

E. MOLLARD, 'Claude Allègre contre le GIEC: De l'arme du faible', *Nature Sciences Sociétés*, 18/2 (2010).

India

D. ADAM, 'Himalayan Glacier Report "Rigorous," Says Martin Parry', *The Hindu* (sourced from *Guardian*), 18 Feb. 2010: http://www.hindu.com/seta/2010/02/18/stories/2010021850011500.htm

S. BILLET, 'Dividing Climate Change: Global Warming in the Indian Mass Media', *Climatic Change*, 99/1–2 (2009), 1–16.

M. BOYKOFF, 'Indian Media Representations of Climate Change in a Threatened Journalistic Ecosystem', *Climatic Change*, 99 (2010), 17–25.

A. DIGHE, 'Disenfranchised and Disempowered: How the Globalized Media Treat their Audiences – A Case from India', in R. S. Fortner and P. M. Fackler (eds), '*The Handbook of Global Communication and Media Ethics*, 2 vols. (Oxford: Wiley-Blackwell, 2011).

A. JOGESH, 'A Change in Climate? Examining Trends in Climate Change Reportage in the Indian Print Media', in Navroz K. Dubash (ed.), *Handbook on Climate Change and India: Development, Politics and Governance* (Oxford and New Delhi: Oxford University Press, forthcoming).

MACRAE, P., 'Increasingly Literate India Fuels Newspaper Boom', *Agence France-Presse*, 16 Sept. 2010: http://www.google.com/hostednews/afp/article/ALeqM5iWiGWdZ6MSHj2m_jjhwuU-_2NlKw

USA

JULIE HOLLAR, '"Climategate" Overshadows Copenhagen: Media Regress to the Bad Old Days of False Balance', FAIR, Feb. 2010: http://www.fair.org/index.php?page=4006.

MATTHEW NISBET, 'Climate Shift: Clear Vision for the Next Decade of Public Debate', American University School of Communication, 2011.

Acknowledgements

Enormous gratitude goes to the researchers for each of the five countries other than the United Kingdom: Anu Jogesh for India, Rebecca Nadin and Yang Di of the British Council for China, Carlos Henrique Fioravanti for Brazil, Kheira Belkacem for France, and Lucy McAllister for the USA. Rebecca Nadin in particular wrote most of the material on China. Many people volunteered insightful comments on these chapters including Claudio Angelo and Gustavo Faleiros (Brazil), Yves Sciama (France), Lavanya Rajamani (India), and Sam Geall (China). Many thanks should be extended to all the journalists and editors in these countries who found time to answer the questionnaires.

Several others were interviewed for the study. Andy Revkin and Curtis Brainard were very helpful in the US sections, while several journalists and editors were interviewed for the UK section. Only parts of their answers have been used, and the rest has been stored up for future use. They include Ben Jackson, Fiona Harvey, Damian Carrington, Mike Swain, Steve Connor, John Ingham, Roger Highfield, and Charles Clover. Benny Peiser was also most helpful.

Others to have helped in differing amounts are Bob Ward, Myanna Lahsen, Max Boykoff, Ricardo Garcia, Graham Lawton, Robert Picard, Lorraine Whitmarsh, Stefan Rahmstorf, Cristiane Azevedo, Tony Giddens, Greg Wilesmith, Paddy Coulter, and Fiona Fox.

The staff of the RISJ offered immensely useful comments, and particularly Rasmus Nielsen and David Levy. Sara Kalim and Alex Reid have been their usual supportive selves. Last but not least, my family has once again put up with the demands of a publication about climate change. My wife Sophia, and two daughters, Maya and Cassie, were even dragooned into helping with comments, pieces of research, and design.

However, as ever, all errors of judgement or fact are mine.